Half Moon Bay Exploring

Nancy M. and Neil A. Evans
Illustrations by Robert R. Dvorak

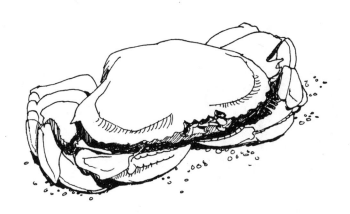

Cover illustration by Robert R. Dvorak

Cover design by Annie Kook
www.infographex.com

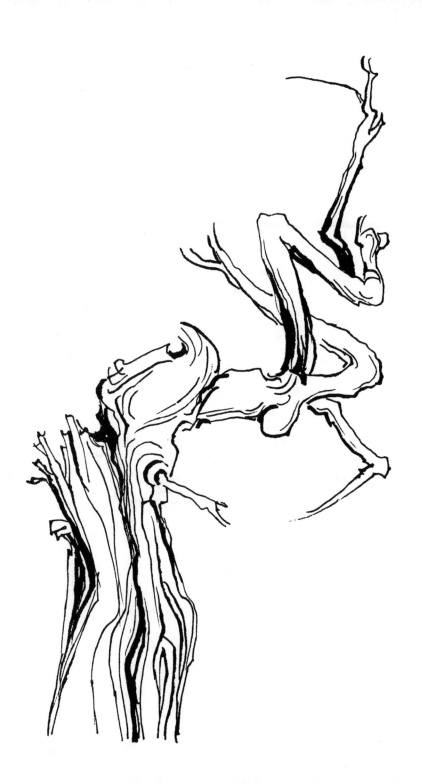

HALF MOON BAY
EXPLORING

Nancy M. and Neil A. Evans
Illustrations by Robert R. Dvorák

Worldview Associates, Inc.
El Granada, California

Half Moon Bay Exploring

Previous edition published under the title *Exploring Half Moon Bay and the San Mateo Coast* text Copyright © 1992, by Nancy M. Evans and Neil A. Evans

Illustrations Copyright © 1992, 1999 by Robert Regis Dvorak

Publisher's Cataloging-in-Publication Data

Evans, Nancy M. and Neil A.

       Half Moon Bay Exploring: the San Mateo Coast - Revised ed.

       Includes index.

       1. Half Moon Bay (Calif.)-Description and travels-Guidebooks. I. Title

Library of Congress Catalog Card Number: 99-90221

ISBN: 0-9632143-4-9

Printed in the United States of America

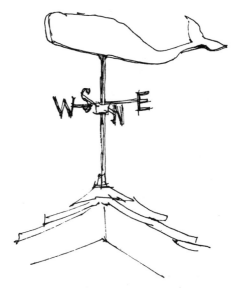

CONTENTS

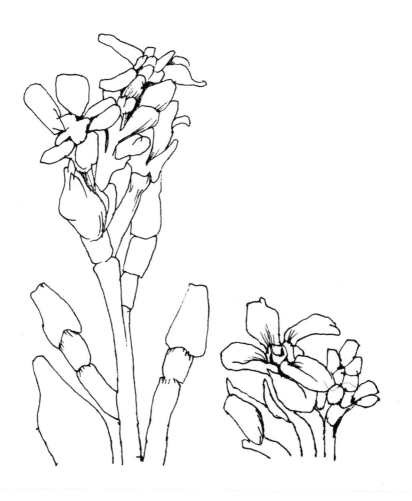

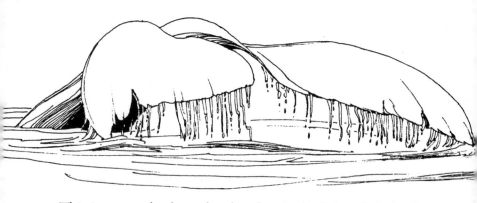

This is a completely updated and revised edition. We thank our readers for corrections and additions which we have incorporated into this book. We have personally visited all entries in this guide. Every effort has been made to ensure that all information is accurate, however, details can change rapidly. We encourage your continued correspondence.

Nancy and Neil Evans

THE AUTHORS

Nancy M. Evans and Neil A. Evans have lived on the California coast for the last 20 years. They are co-authors of *Monterey Peninsula Exploring*. Nancy Evans has worked in the travel industry for many years. Neil Evans is a professor of international business at San Francisco State University and has written on tourism, international business and environmental issues.

THE ARTIST

Robert Regis Dvorak is an artist and illustrator for *Monterey Peninsula Exploring* and a professional speaker on the subject of creativity in business and education. He is the author of four books on drawing: *The Magic of Drawing, Experiential Drawing, Drawing without Fear,* and *The Pocket Drawing Book.* He resides in Half Moon Bay.

MAP OF BEACHES

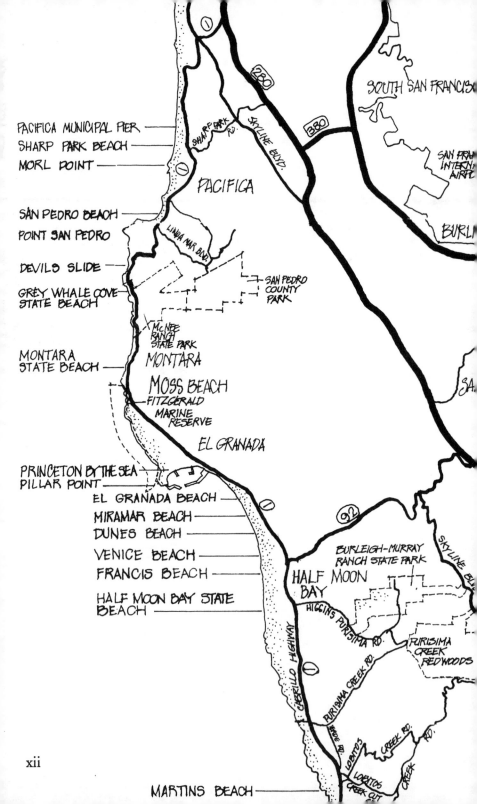

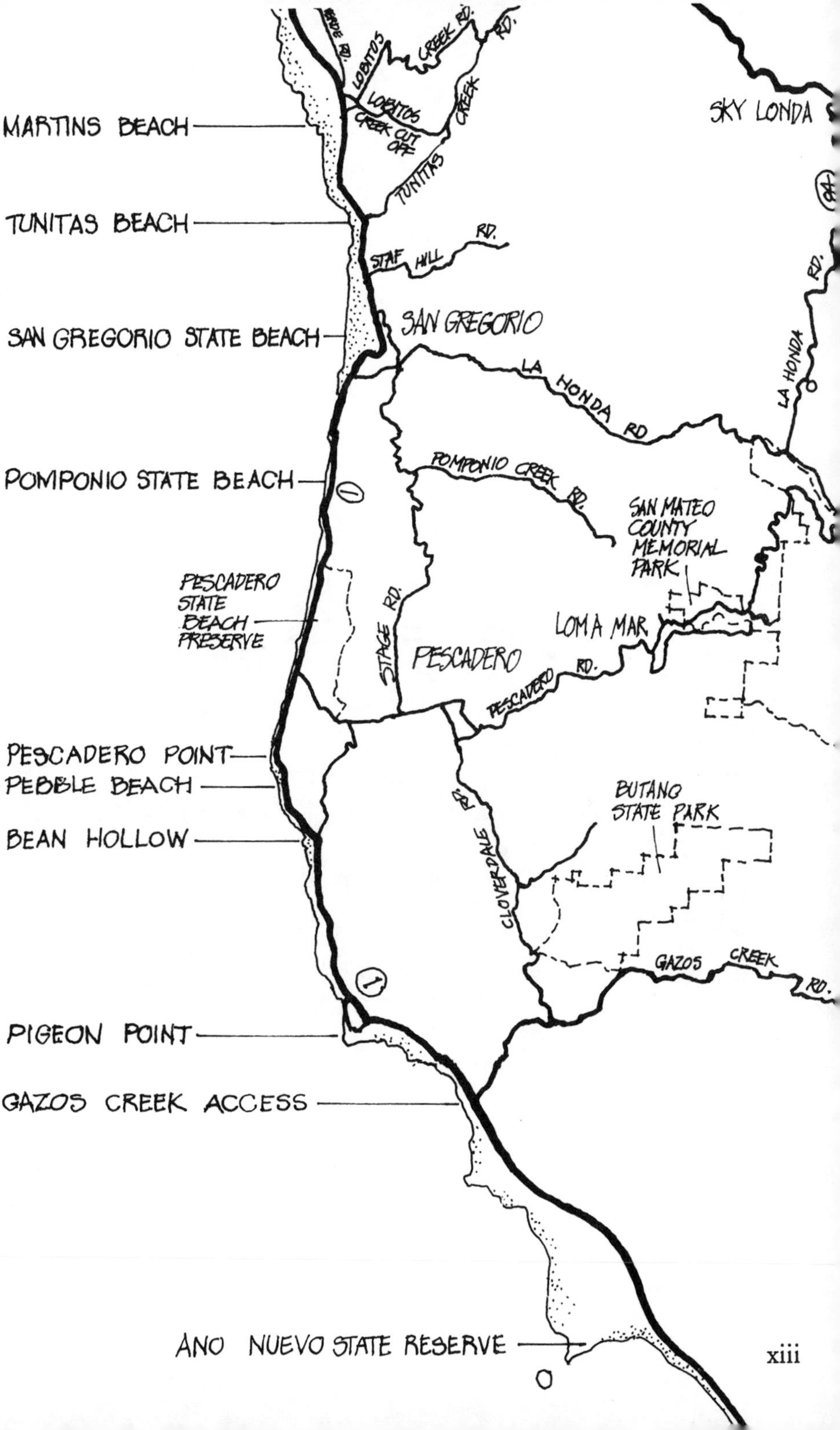

MARTINS BEACH

TUNITAS BEACH

SAN GREGORIO STATE BEACH

POMPONIO STATE BEACH

PESCADERO STATE BEACH PRESERVE

PESCADERO POINT
PEBBLE BEACH

BEAN HOLLOW

PIGEON POINT

GAZOS CREEK ACCESS

ANO NUEVO STATE RESERVE

SKY LONDA

SAN GREGORIO

SAN MATEO COUNTY MEMORIAL PARK

LOMA MAR

PESCADERO

BUTANO STATE PARK

LOBITOS CREEK RD.

LOBITOS CREEK CUT OFF

TUNITAS CREEK

STAGE HILL RD.

LA HONDA RD.

LA HONDA RD.

POMPONIO CREEK RD.

STAGE RD.

PESCADERO RD.

CLOVERDALE RD.

GAZOS CREEK RD.

xiii

Romeo's Pier, Princeton-by-the-Sea

1

INTRODUCING

Face west and the blue, gray, and green of the Pacific greets the eye. Turn east and one of the most pleasing jumbles of coastal cliffs, mountains, farmland and small village-like towns comes into view. The San Mateo County coast, south of San Francisco, is one of the most geographically compelling and attractive spots in California.

Where else in the world can you experience such a wide diversity of nature? It is bound on the west by the Pacific Ocean, sharp dramatic cliffs, white sandy beaches; and on the east by the coastal mountains, high chaparral, stands of redwoods, and shady glens of ferns. In between lies some of California's best farmland, covered with fields of artichokes, Brussels sprouts, pumpkins, peas, and cut flowers.

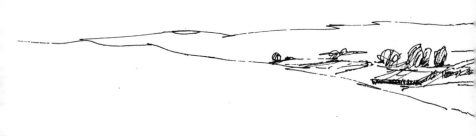

Three distinct regions make up the Coastside:

Half Moon Bay is the heart of the area. Together with the northern Mid-Coast communities of El Granada, Miramar, Princeton-by-the-Sea, Moss Beach and Montara, it is known simply as the "Coastside" by the local population.

South of Half Moon Bay are San Gregorio, Pescadero, La Honda, Año Nuevo, and the vast beauty and blend of beaches, mountains, and farmland. Most people refer to this region as the South Coast.

Pacifica is the northernmost community and is separated from the other coastal towns by Devil's Slide and four miles of a rugged Mediterranean-like coastline.

WEATHER
Most visitors who come to the Coastside during the summer are familiar with the high fog blowing off the ocean, bringing a natural air conditioning to the area. Generally, the persistent fog rolls in around July 15 and rolls out again around September 15; frequently there are two to three days of fog followed by one bright sunny day.

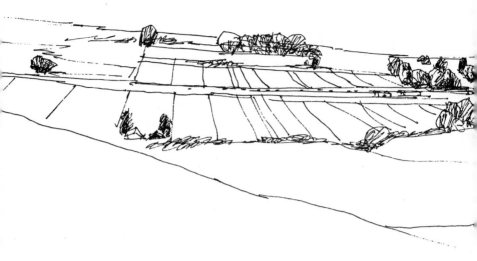

A secret to residents and knowledgeable visitors is that the weather is at its best during the fall and winter months. When it is foggy and cold on the other side of the mountain, the sun often is shining down on the ocean, and the beaches are refreshingly empty.

Except for a few days a year, when the temperatures climb into the 80's or drop below 40°F, the weather stays between a moderate 62°F and 47°F, making it perfect for year-round enjoyment of many sports activities.

POPULATION
According to the latest census data, the total population of the Coast from Pacifica to Año Nuevo is 60,996. The population of Pacifica makes up the bulk of this at 37,670. The Coastside from Montara to Tunitas Creek, south of Half Moon Bay, has a population of 18,866; 8,886 of these inhabitants live within the Half Moon Bay city limits. The area of San Gregorio, Pescadero, and south to the county line is home to 4,460. This is an ethnically diverse population mainly composed of Anglo-Europeans, Hispanics, Portuguese, Italians, and Japanese.

USING THIS BOOK

Unless otherwise noted, each chapter of the book begins with the natural focus of the area, which is Half Moon Bay, followed by the northern Mid-Coast communities. South Coast entries follow, and the Pacifica commentary concludes each section.

The **Remembering Chapter** is a brief historic sketch of the role and impact of the early contributors: Indians, Spanish explorers, pioneers, farmers, artisans, and entrepreneurs.

Historic highlights of the Coastside form the **Seeing Chapter**. Poke around downtown Half Moon Bay and Pescadero to find clues of life in the late 1800's by visiting the historic buildings and picturesque graveyards. Go back further in time, to the days of the Ohlone Indians, at the Sanchez Adobe in Pacifica. There are two lighthouses that lighten the coast, a working harbor at Pillar Point, and a fishing pier in Pacifica to explore.

The **Adventuring Chapter** details the natural phenomena of the area: beaches, parks, and mountains. Several shining stars stand out: Mavericks, the infamous Northern California big wave; the James V. Fitzgerald Marine Reserve, one of the best places in California to view tide pool life; Año Nuevo State Reserve, home to an elephant seal population; and Sweeney Ridge, discovery site of San Francisco Bay. Coastal parks and beaches are described; the best places to find wildflowers, watch birds and butterflies, and to spot whales are noted.

Hike along the bluffs, up over a mountain or under the redwoods. Bike along the Coastside Trail, through Pillar Point Harbor, or in back of Sharp Park Golf Course. Kayak in the harbor, fish from the pier or from a deep sea fishing boat, golf right along the ocean's edge. The wide variety of sporting activities available are in the **Sporting Chapter**.

Cultural activities are highlighted in the **Entertaining Chapter.** Plays, jazz, rock, country, comedy, classical? The coastside has them all. In addition, yearly celebrations are held to honor pumpkins, fishing, flowers, the Portuguese population, and even the fog. People meet for all kinds of reasons: weddings, picnics, company get-togethers. The best places along the coast for such activities are also found in this chapter.

The Coastside is blessed with an unusual number of outstanding bed and breakfasts, motels, hostels, and camping facilities. Every place from an elegant manor house to a lighthouse youth hostel are described and pinpointed by community in the **Sleeping Chapter.** For dining possibilities and a description of the many diverse restaurants of the area, see **Eating.**

A variety of shopping prospects exist in the coastal communities. Boutiques have mushroomed on Main Street, Half Moon Bay, making it a destination shopping area. The smaller towns of Pescadero, La Honda, and Davenport are also worth a peek. Looking for produce? The coast is a cornucopia of fruits, vegetables, Christmas trees, and, of course, pumpkins. The best of nature's bounty can be found in the **Shopping Chapter.**

Join us in this varied setting. Refresh your mind and body with long walks on the beach, reel in your limit of salmon, gallop on horseback in the surf, pick the perfect pumpkin from field or stand, and hike under a canopy of redwood trees to absorb their majesty. It is little wonder that approximately three million people a year come to this unique landscape; it is worthy of many return visits.

The area code for San Mateo County is 650

A statue of Portolá, located at
the corner of Highway 1 and
Crespi Drive in Pacifica, reads:
Captain Don Gaspar de Portolá
born in Balaguer, Catalonia, Spain.
First governor of California, founder
of San Diego and Monterey.
Discoverer of the Bay of San Francisco
on November 4, 1769. Presented
by the President of the Generalitat
of Catalonia, The Honorable Jordi
Pujol, on November 5, 1988, to
the people of the state of California,
the Honorable George Deukmejian,
Governor.

2

REMEMBERING

The history of the San Mateo coast is a mirror-image of the whole of California. A rich land and a diversity of landscape have lured, first, the Ohlone Indians and then waves of European, Hispanic, and Asian settlers. The interplay of land and people continues to this day and has contributed to an intriguing historic story.

EXPLORERS

Spanish explorers led by Gaspar de Portolá marched through what we now call the San Mateo coast in 1769 while looking for Monterey Bay. The scenery and climate were reminiscent of Spain to Portolá's band, and the politics of the day suggested to Portolá that he claim the area in the name of the Spanish crown.

When the group climbed to the top of **Sweeney Ridge** (in Pacifica), Portolá and his followers sighted what we now know as San Francisco Bay. It was the first recorded discovery of the famous water landmark.

After Mexico won its independence from Spain, the Mexican Government parceled out the land for vast ranchos. San Benito was one of the little towns to emerge. Nicknamed Spanishtown, it was later changed to Half Moon Bay. The northern section of the San Mateo coast became a fertile growing ground for fruits, vegetables, and meat for Mission Dolores in San Francisco. Later, Don Francisco Sanchez was deeded this area as his private rancho. We can find a reminder of this in the refurbished **Sanchez Adobe**, situated in Pacifica.

The New York, a three-masted iron ship built in 1883, shipwrecked in Half Moon Bay on March 13, 1898.

SETTLERS

Throughout the next decades of immigration and development Italian farmers, Portuguese fishermen and whalers, Anglo lumbermen, Irish dairymen, German merchants, and Japanese flower growers settled and added to the rich ethnic diversity of the Coastside.

The coastal mountain range and the proximity of the Pacific pinched in efforts to develop an efficient transportation system. Those roads that were built were steep, hazardous, and an ongoing impediment to the easy movement of people and goods. The logical answer seemed to be the development of wharves for shipping up and down the coast and on to the important San Francisco market.

WHARVES AND SHIPS

One wharf after another sprouted up along the San Mateo coast. A seemingly ingenious idea was known as Gordon's Chute (at Tunitas Creek bluff) where cargo was sent plummeting down a 45 degree slide from the cliff to the ships below. In the end, a storm dismantled the chute and ended the ill-conceived scheme.

The rocky shoreline and the fog were just as troublesome for ships and boats as the mountainous landscape had been for the building of roads. Many ships were wrecked as they tried to work their way to the small wharves. From 1850 to 1950 more than sixty ships were badly damaged or destroyed along the San Mateo coast.

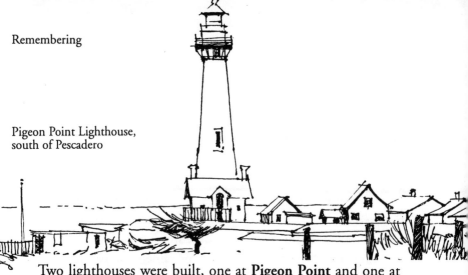

Pigeon Point Lighthouse,
south of Pescadero

Two lighthouses were built, one at **Pigeon Point** and one at
Point Montara, and were of assistance in providing warning
beacon-lights to passing ships. But it wasn't until better roads
were constructed and automobiles and trucks plentiful that
farmers could safely take their merchandise to market.

Montara itself was a dreamed-of artist colony and to this day
retains an artist-in-residence quality. Meanwhile, Moss Beach
had become a center for the scientific study of the impressive
tidepools and great "mosses" that washed up on the shore.

OCEAN SHORE RAILROAD
To encourage tourism development and the building of seaside cabins and houses, the Ocean Shore Railroad Company
was established in 1905. The company had an ambitious plan
to turn much of the Coastside into a coastal resort and mecca.
The railroad started in San Francisco and ran along a coastal
route through small villages that later became Pacifica, it hugged
the mountain at Devil's Slide, and traveled south through
Montara, Moss Beach, El Granada, and Half Moon Bay. The
route ended at Tunitas Creek, south of Half Moon Bay. A
Stanley Steamer picked up those adventurous travelers who
wished to motor further south down the coast.

The hub of this tourist paradise was to be El Granada. Famed
town planner, D.H. Burnham, laid out a series of semicircles

and wide boulevards in an effort to capture a European-like ambiance. Thousands of trees were planted and sidewalks poured throughout the town-to-be. Unfortunately for the Ocean Shore Railroad Company, many trainloads of prospective buyers came but few actually bought property in El Granada, and the dream of a tourist center died. The semicircle roads and the sidewalks of El Granada remain today as distinguishing features of the forgotten plan.

The Ocean Shore plan failed, and the railroad track was dug up in the 1920's. Even the resort communities of San Gregorio and Pescadero lost favor with vacationers. But the isolated beach coves and relatively deserted roads became perfect covers for a new population—the rumrunners and bootleggers of Prohibition days. When Prohibition was repealed, most of the Coastside returned to its sleepy agrarian ways. By contrast, Pacifica, with its easy access to San Francisco, developed by leaps and bounds. To this day, Pacifica has better developed roads and is far more urbanized than the rest of the San Mateo County coast.

DEVELOPMENT

By the early 1970's the issue of coastal development began to have an important political effect. In 1972, California voters, tired of rampant coast despoliation, passed the Coastal Initiative and created the Coastal Act. The Act literally stopped land development in its tracks and set forth stringent conditions for future building. Despite its proximity to a major megalopolis, the relative preservation of the San Mateo coast was an immense environmental accomplishment.

The decades of the 1980's and 1990's mark a continuing struggle between preservationists and developmental interests. We have come full circle—the San Mateo coast mirrors the whole of California.

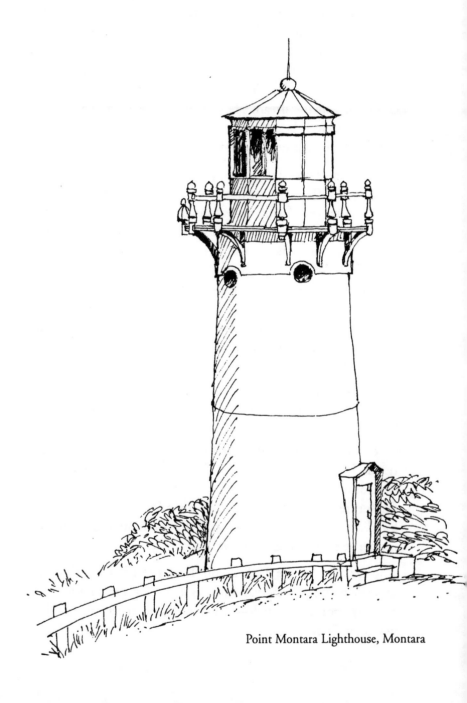

Point Montara Lighthouse, Montara

3

SEEING

If you enjoy natural beauty and historic sites the Coastside is a delightful discovery. A walking tour of Half Moon Bay's Main Street yields old-time buildings and a pleasurable sense of the past. Pescadero resembles nothing so much as a small western town. There is even a noted saloon to round out the impression of the old west. A visit to the Sanchez Adobe in Pacifica takes the visitor even further back in California history to the days of ranchos and Spanish dons. Lighthouses at Pigeon Point in the south and Point Montara in the north are picturesque reminders that the San Mateo coast is one of the most beautiful coastlines anywhere.

This chapter is a guide to historic and man-made highlights and begins with sights in **Half Moon Bay**, followed by those on the **Mid-Coast**, the **South Coast**, and **Pacifica**. Parks, beaches, and the great outdoors are covered in Chapter 4, the Adventuring chapter.

HALF MOON BAY

Historic Half Moon Bay

If you are an enthusiast of well-preserved buildings and historic small towns, your interest will be rewarded by a walk through downtown Half Moon Bay, the oldest town in San Mateo County. The Spanishtown Historical Society provides walking-tour maps that can be purchased at local stores, the Chamber of Commerce, 520 Kelly Avenue, or at the Spanishtown Historical Society headquartered at the **Old Jail**, 505 Johnston Street, open from 12 p.m. to 3 p.m., Friday, Saturday, and Sunday. For guided walking tours of historic downtown Half Moon Bay write the Spanishtown Historical Society at P.O. Box 62, Half Moon Bay, CA 94019.

Two of the town's most notable buildings are listed on the National Register of Historic Places. One, the **James Johnston House**, is prominently situated on a knoll overlooking prime farmland. The salt-box style building was constructed in 1855, which is belied by its renovated bright white paint job. The Johnston House is a museum in progress, open for tours on request. It is located on Higgins Purisima Road off Highway l, just south of Half Moon Bay. For additional information call the Johnston House Foundation at 726-0329; school groups call the San Mateo County Historical Association at 299-0104.

James Johnston House, Half Moon Bay

Community United Methodist Church,
Half Moon Bay

The **Community United Methodist Church**, on the corner of
Johnston and Miramontes Streets, was built in 1872 and is
also on the Historic Register. The white-boarded church has
blue trim, a bell tower, and stained glass windows, each repre-
senting a different hymn. The church is not grandly impos-
ing, but provides a comforting human scale. Open for tours
upon arrangement. 726-4621.

The **Zaballa House** at 324 Main Street was constructed in 1859 and is the oldest building in town still in use. It is a classic, early California wooden building and has been stylishly converted into a coastal-colored powder-blue bed and breakfast. The **San Benito House**, at 356 Main Street, has the look and the history of an old coaching inn and indeed is the former Mosconi Hotel. A restaurant and recreated westernstyle saloon add to the old California atmosphere.

San Benito House,
Half Moon Bay

Cunha's Country Store, a two-story building that looks like it came straight from a western movie set, guards the corner of Main Street and Kelly Avenue, and has been a general merchandise store since 1900. The **Half Moon Bay Bakery**, at 514 Main Street, still uses its original brick ovens for making bread. Try some and enjoy a winning picnic in the nearby Mac Dutra Park, a pocket-sized town-square.

The **Pilarcitos Cemetery** on Highway 92 is just east of Main Street and dates from the mid 1800's; you can find the tombstones of many of the town's pioneers such as members of the Johnston family.

The Victorian style blue and white **Alves House** is prominently situated at 520 Kelly Avenue, and houses the Half Moon Bay Chamber of Commerce (726-5202).

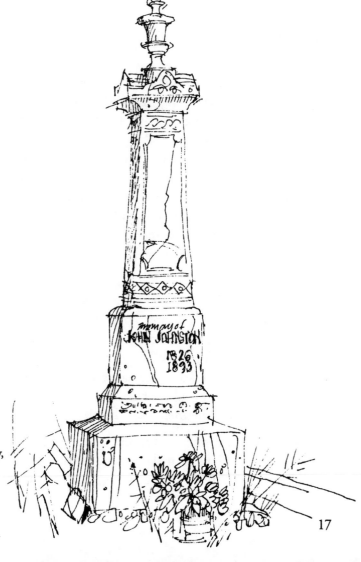

Tombstone from
Pilarcitos Cemetery,
Half Moon Bay

MID-COAST

Pillar Point Harbor

The relatively seamless California coast has few protective points or prominent outcroppings. But Pillar Point is one of them. At night, with its string of lights, it looks like the largest battleship in the American fleet. Atop the point is a scattering of buildings housing the Pillar Point Air Force Station. This radar tracking station is not open to the public. Beneath its protective presence sits Pillar Point Harbor, the only harbor between San Francisco and Santa Cruz. This natural port has been used by coastal fishermen for centuries, but the harbor, with its tracings of rip-rap breakwaters, was first constructed in 1961 and then enhanced with inner breakwaters in 1982.

The harbor has a clash of boats. The maze of commercial fishing vessels with their ungainly appearance and too cute names (Susie Q's and Mary Jo's) contrast with the sleek recreational yachts with their dominant blue canvas and white hulls. Walk Johnson Pier and take in the cacophony of fishing activity. Watch fishermen unload their catch, work their nets, and dock their boats. The fishermen look like, well, fishermen.

The number of commercial fishing boats is declining as it becomes more difficult to make a living in fishing, but they still land about 10 million tons of fish annually. During most of

the year, fish are sold directly from the boats. A commercial abalone farming operation is located off shore.

Circle the harbor by foot and see the many possibilities for seaside and ocean activity. These include party fishing boats, whale watching tours, ramps for launching boats, picnic tables, fishing off the pier for the delicacies of the harbor, restaurants and their chalk-boarded "catch of the day," and paths and roads that circle the harbor. It is classic harbor activity. West of Highway 1 on Capistrano Road in Princeton. Harbormaster: 726-5727 or 726-4382. For weather updates call: 726-6070. Website: www.smchd.dst.ca.us. SEE: Sporting chapter for additional information.

Point Montara Lighthouse
For those who picture lighthouses as tall cylindrical beacons, Point Montara is a surprise. It is a lighthouse in miniature, short and squat. Point Montara is located on a high rocky point, a very impressive setting. The grounds include an old barn, formerly used to store oil, that has been converted into a meeting or party facility. Adjacent coastal Victorian buildings accommodate a youth hostel. The lighthouse is open daily from 7:30 to 10:30 a.m. and from 4:30 to 9:30 p.m. Located at 16th Street and Highway 1 in Montara. 728-7177. Website: www.norcalhostels.org. SEE: Sleeping chapter for further information on the youth hostel.

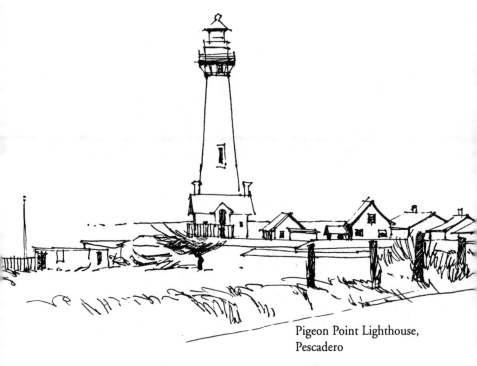

Pigeon Point Lighthouse,
Pescadero

SOUTH COAST

Pigeon Point Lighthouse

Pigeon Point Lighthouse is one of the area's local TV stars. The classic and stately sentry has been used as a set piece in television commercials. The beacon was constructed in 1872 after several ships crashed into the rocks at Pigeon Point. At 115 feet it is quite monumental and is one of the tallest lighthouses on the West Coast. Join a tour and view the original first-order Fresnel (pronounced fra-nel) lens and its 1,008 glass prisms, all of which are still in place. The light from the tower is visible from eighteen to twenty miles.

For those looking for an overnight stop, a forty-bed hostel is a part of the lighthouse complex. A full day's activity is an easy possibility. The tidepools and surf fishing just north will occupy the avid beach goer and fisherman. Or, see gray whales,

humpback whales, harbor seals, elephant seals, otters, sea lions, and sea birds. Lighthouse tours are given on Saturday and Sunday between 10 a.m. and 3 p.m. No public restrooms for beach goers. The facilities are open from 7:30 to 9:30 a.m. and 4:30 to 9:00 p.m. Located seven-miles south of Pescadero, off Highway 1. 879-0633. Website: www.norcalhostels.org. SEE: Sleeping chapter for additional information.

Historic Pescadero
Once a resort area, Pescadero on the surface looks like it belongs in a western movie. Local residents fiercely protect this image in an effort to save their part of the coast from development. A complete Pescadero walking-tour book can be purchased at local stores and will prove invaluable for your stroll down Stage Road, the main street of town. Notable are **Duarte's Tavern** looking like a "cowboy hangout;" Country Roads, an antique store in a barn; and Arcangeli's market with aromas of fresh from the oven bread.

Community Church,
Pescadero

Historic churches and a cemetery mark the Pescadero landscape. The **Methodist Episcopal Church** on Stage Road is on
the National Registry of Historic Places; the **Pescadero
Community Church**, located on Stage Road, was built in 1867,
and is the oldest Protestant church on the San Francisco Peninsula; **Saint Anthony's Catholic Church**, on North Street,
was built in 1870. The **Mt. Hope/St Anthony's Cemetery** on
Stage Road has been the burial grounds for Pescadero residents since the 1860's.

La Honda

Relive the 1960s by taking Highway 84 to La Honda. Revisit images of Ken Kesey and his Merry Pranksters immortalized in Tom Wolfe's book "The Electric Cool Aid Acid Test." La Honda is a redwood tree-surrounded village loaded with charm and local lore. After the 1906 earthquake, the redwood forests were heavily logged for timber to rebuild San Francisco. The town retains both the logging camp and hippy atmosphere of its past. **Apple Jacks,** a local bar and popular stop for the motorcycle crowd, was built in 1879 and offers live musical entertainment on the weekends. Follow Highway 84 up to Skyline Blvd to the **Kings Mountain Country Store**, 13100 Skyline (851-3852). Here you will find a wonderful history wall depicting life in early La Honda area, as well as a wide selection of local wines, toys, and other dry goods.

Davenport

The cement mining town cum artist's colony of Davenport looks like nothing more than a wide spot on Highway 1, but this town contains more than first meets the eye. The **Davenport Jail,** located a block from Highway 1 and built in 1914, no longer houses local miscreants, only historic exhibits of the coastal region. Park your car by the jail and begin your walking tour of Davenport. To the north there is a restaurant, grocery store, and a very fine art glass shop. To the south, is the **Davenport Cash Store**, Restaurant and Inn. To the east, are streets lined with clapboard houses and **St. Vincent de Paul Catholic Church**, constructed in 1915 by local workers from local materials. SEE: The Shopping chapter for some outstanding craft shops. To the west, on the ocean bluffs, is a premiere perch for watching the migrating gray whales. Davenport is located thirty-eight miles south of Half Moon Bay.

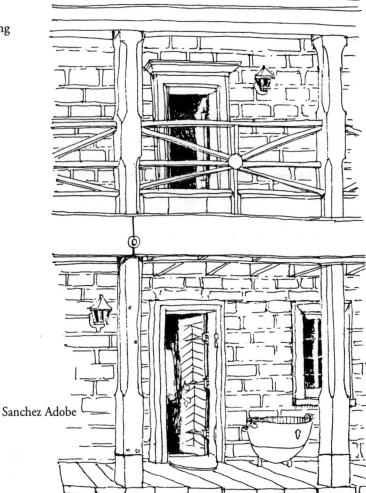

Sanchez Adobe

PACIFICA

The Sanchez Adobe

The adobe of Don Francisco Sanchez, built in 1846, immediately transports you into old California. Envision a Spanish-style adobe building of classic early California design, authentically refurbished rooms filled with historic furniture, clothing, and tools from the days of Spanish rule of California. Fix this picture in your mind, you will capture the Sanchez Adobe as it now stands, saved from its earlier day hard use as a hotel and speakeasy. You can tour this restored adobe, now a state historic landmark, and view relics of the Ohlone Indians as well as the artifacts of the Spanish rancho days. It is open Tuesday and Thursday 10 a.m. to 4 p.m.; Saturday and Sunday 1 to 5 p.m Located at 1000 Linda Mar Blvd, about one mile east of Highway l. 359-1462. SEE: Remembering chapter for more information.

Pacifica Municipal Pier

This concrete modern pier takes a narrow but significant bite into the Pacific. At over 1,000 feet long it juts out from a landscaped beach-side area at Sharp Park Beach. Fishing for striped bass, smelt, lingcod, and salmon is good. Whale watching in winter and spring is a possibility. And contemplating Pedro Point Bay and surf hitting the pier and shore is an enjoyable reflective activity. A concession stand has food, drink and fishing supplies, and is at the ready. The pier is open twenty-four hours a day. Restrooms are available. Located on Beach Blvd at Santa Rosa Avenue. 355-0690. SEE: Sporting chapter for more details.

DRIVING TOURS

The coastside offers many possibilities for entertaining "see the landscape" drives; here are two favorites.

Sea Shore Splendor

Distance: forty-one miles: from Pacifica to Año Nuevo along Highway 1, this is one of the most spectacular drives in Northern California.

Begin your drive in Pacifica, on Highway 1 at Highway 35, for an unsurpassed bird's-eye view of the coastline. A stop at San Pedro Beach is in order, to watch the surfers and take in the ambiance. Continue south on Highway 1, along Devil's Slide where the sharp cliffy terrain is reminiscent of the Amalfi Coast in Italy. If it is a clear day, the Faralone Islands can be seen twenty-five miles off shore. The sandy expanse of Montara

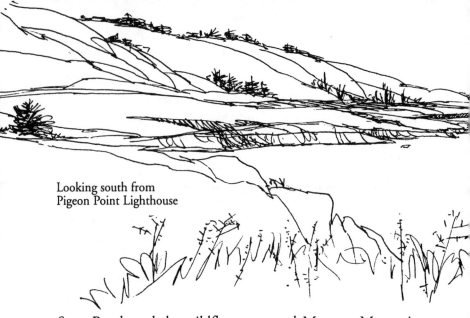

Looking south from
Pigeon Point Lighthouse

State Beach and the wildflower-covered Montara Mountain form the northern gateway to the mid-coast. There are numerous stops one could make in the towns of Montara, Moss Beach, and El Granada. We suggest a short stop at Pillar Point Harbor in Princeton-by-the-Sea for a walk on the pier and perhaps a bowl of clam chowder. South of Half Moon Bay, farm land becomes one of the prominent features. Fields of artichokes lead to the edge of bluffs above the crashing waves. There are a number of beach-access trails through the fields marked with brown and yellow signs. Stay on the trails at all times as they cut through private property.

There are numerous California State Park beaches between Half Moon Bay and Año Nuevo. A favorite is Pebble Beach/ Bean Hollow State Beach, south of Pescadero. Park in the northern-most parking lot and walk the trail south along the bluffs. Continue south to your next stop, the Pigeon Point Lighthouse, for a self-guided tour of this picturesque structure. Año Nuevo State Reserve, about twenty-seven miles south of Half Moon Bay, is your last stop. Between December and April, the elephant seals' breeding season, you will need reservations to visit. The rest of the year self-guided tours are possible.

Farmland/Redwood Forest Circle Route
Distance: twenty-four miles of windy, hilly roads.

Drive south from Half Moon Bay along coastal Highway 1 for ten miles and turn east to San Gregorio and the General Store. Depart San Gregorio traveling east on the San Gregorio Road (Highway 84). Very soon you leave the rolling farm lands, which are replaced by redwoods, cedar, pine and madrone that shade the windy road on the way to La Honda. After a walking tour of La Honda, with perhaps a stop at the La Honda Creations Craft Gallery, backtrack the short distance along Highway 84, and turn onto Pescadero Road. Continue for about one mile, veer left on to Alpine Road. Go about one mile on this very narrow, shady road, to the Heritage Grove car park. To the right of the small parking area, cross the wooden bridge and take one of the hiking trails through this virgin redwood grove. The smell of the bay leaves, the damp forests of ferns and moss covered giant trees give the visitor the sense of pre-logged and forested California.

Backtrack to Alpine Road and continue towards Pescadero. Next stop is Sam McDonald County Park where more hiking trails await the energetic. You will also find picnic tables, barbecue pits, and restrooms. Continue on Pescadero Road, through San Mateo Memorial Park; now the terrain returns to rolling hills doted with farms. As you approach Pescadero, the Phipps Family Farm will be on your left. Stop here to see the farm animals, buy fresh produce, and pick your own berries during the season. Hot bowls of artichoke soup, homemade olallieberry pie, and other local favorites are served at Duartes Tavern in Pescadero, a perfect ending to your tour. Return to San Gregorio, via Old Stage Road, the main street of Pescadero.

4

ADVENTURING

Long expansive beaches, one of the world's biggest surfing waves, renown tidepool and marine life, rare small stone pebble beaches, ideal ocean coves, wind-swept and sea grass covered dunes and more all await visitors to the San Mateo Coast. It does not enjoy the notoriety of the Big Sur area, but in many ways the San Mateo coastline is the equal to its more famous geographic cousin to the south.

Here, we help you explore the major beaches and inland parks of the San Mateo coast. Our journey begins with the Half Moon Bay area. It follows with the Mid-Coast, the South Coast, Pacifica and the North Coast. Last we visit our favorite places to view wildflowers, watch birds, wade in tidepools and spot whales.

MONTEREY BAY NATIONAL MARINE SANCTUARY

Look off shore for America's largest marine sanctuary—larger than any land based national park. The Monterey Bay National Marine Sanctuary ranges from north of San Francisco and south to Big Sur, nearly 150 miles in length, approximately thirty-five miles in width, some 5300 square miles of aquatic sanctuary for hundreds of species of marine mammals, seabirds, fish, amphibians, and plant life. The federal regulations governing the sanctuary prohibits disturbing or removing the protected marine life. For additional information contact the Monterey Bay National Marine Sanctuary at 299 Foam Street, Suite D, Monterey, CA 93940. 408-647-4201. Website: http://bonita.mbnms.nos.noaa.gov.

HALF MOON BAY

Half Moon Bay State Beach

This is one of the best all-purpose beaches along the coast and is blessed with all the favorite attributes of beach going. The entire four-mile stretch of beach from Half Moon Bay to Pillar Point Harbor is broad and sandy and good for families and

Half Moon Bay Beach

individuals alike. Surf fishing, beach combing, surfing, walk-
ing, and picnicking are all available. The main access points
are Francis Beach, Dunes Beach, Venice Beach, and Roosevelt
Beach, all off Highway 1 between Half Moon Bay and Miramar.
All are administered by the California State Department of
Parks and Recreation. 726-8820. Website: www.park-net.com.

Francis Beach
Francis Beach, one of the most impressive view beaches in the
area, overlooks the arch of Half Moon Bay. This is a good
surfing and family activities beach and offers the following:
overnight camping for tents and RV's, wheelchair-accessible
restrooms, outdoor cold showers, barbecues, and picnic tables.
There is also a weekly campfire program. Fifty-one sites are
available for tents and RV's with no RV hook-ups. Parking
and overnight fees. Turn west at the stop light on Highway 1
and Kelly Avenue. No reservations: first come-first served. SEE:
Sleeping chapter for more information.

Venice, Dunes, and Roosevelt Beaches

These beaches are located between Half Moon Bay and Miramar and are clearly marked on Highway 1. They offer typical beach activities on wide gently sloping shores; Dunes Beach provides a rarity for the California beach goer: sea grass-covered dunes. Parking lot and restrooms are available. Entrance fees.

Cowell Ranch State Park

Cowell Ranch State Park, one of the newest additions to the state park system, is also one of the smallest. The park is comprised of 1200 linear feet of ocean front and approximately fourteen acres of bluff top overlooks. A dirt road through fields of Brussels spouts takes you to a bluff vista point over looking a pristine sandy beach cove. Steep stairs descend to the beach and ocean. To the south, (not accessible) is a stretch of beach reserved for sea lions and other marine mammals. The Cowell Ranch State Park parking lot is located on Highway 1, about three miles south of Highway 92. 726-8819.

Burleigh Murray Ranch State Park

Stroll through old California in this 1300 acre state park. Take in the California countryside with its rolling hills, mixed stands of trees (including huge eucalyptus lining the path), a meandering creek, and pleasant vistas of the landscape. Hike or bike two miles on a level road to a former dairy and the well preserved remains of an old, rambling English-style bank barn set against a hillside. This is one of the few English bank barns built on the West Coast. Hay was pitched from the top bank level to the cattle entering the barn on the ground level. Antique farm implements and atmospheric old stonework walls complete the trip to the past. Turn left at the ranger's house to see the bank barn. Additional hiking trails, picnic tables, and restrooms are available. Turn east from Highway 1 on to Higgins Purisima Road, south of Half Moon Bay. The parking lot is on the left about 1 ¼ miles. SEE: Sporting chapter for additional information.

Bank Barn
Burleigh Murray Ranch State Park

Purisima Creek Redwoods Open Space Preserve
Local residents escape the summer fog by visiting the redwood groves and winding creek in this 2500 acre park. Here is the place to revisit the sun. Hike the twenty miles of developed trails; several begin just past the entrance gate where there is a wooden map detailing the various trails. Some trails are for mountain bikers and equestrians. Turn east on Higgins Purisima Road just south of Half Moon Bay on Highway 1. Go about four miles to the entrance gate and a small parking lot nestled in the trees beside a small bridge. The other entrance to the Preserve, and the trailhead to the Whittemore Gulch Trail, is on Highway 35, Skyline Blvd, about 4 ½ miles south of Highway 92. The one-fourth mile Redwood Trail is wheelchair accessible and begins at the parking lot off Highway 35 about 6 ½ miles south of Highway 92. Restrooms and picnic tables are available. Website: www.openspace.org. SEE: Sporting chapter for additional information.

Half Moon Bay City Parks
The Parks and Recreation Department of Half Moon Bay maintains several pocket parks throughout the city. Three are in downtown Half Moon Bay and are good spots for picnics: John L. Carter Park is a grassy oasis located down some steps near the Stone Pine Center parking lot, off Main Street; MacDutra Park, on the corner of Main Street and Kelly Avenue, and Kitty Fernandez Park, located on Main and Filbert Streets, are both brick-patio parks.

MID-COAST

Pillar Point Harbor
SEE: Seeing and Sporting chapters for harbor information.

Mavericks

When the surf is up, world class surfers descend on Mavericks, the infamous Northern California big wave hidden on the backside of the radar station at Princeton-by-the-Sea. Only the best surfers dare to ride the thirty-foot waves; but on good days galleries of spectators line the bluffs to catch a glance, if not a wave. Off Highway 1, turn onto Capistrano Road in Princeton, take any street, and drive towards the radar station on the hill. Turn right on West Point and continue to the small parking lot. The paved road to the radar station is off limits. Surfers, and beach-side viewers, should following the trail around the left side of the station. For the best views of Mavericks, climb the steep cliff on the far left side of the radar station and edge around the cyclone fence. For a slightly more accessible bluff view, climb the hill on the right side of the radar station. Mavericks is located about one mile off shore, slightly north of the radar station site. Website: www.HMBSurfco.com.

West Shoreline Access

The Pillar Point Wetlands is a salt marsh habitat and the West Shoreline Access is a path skirting past the wetlands and around the backside of the radar station. The trail hugs the harbor, lending far off views of the coast range and close-up views of shorebirds and novice kayakers. Walk around the end of the point to the pounding open ocean surf and kelp strewn coast. This cove conjures up images of rum runners and pirates. Off to the far right, behind the jagged rocks just off shore, you can see Mavericks, one of the best surfing spots in the world. Restroom and unpaved parking lot available. See directions to Mavericks above. Park in the lot provided or walk from other approved parking spots. The police are diligent in giving tickets for illegally parked vehicles.

El Granada Beach

Surfers not quite up to Maverick's big swells, can catch the waves south of the Pillar Point Harbor jetty at El Granada Beach, popular with surfers, wind surfers, jet skiers and virtually everyone, judging by week-end crowds. For those less inclined to surf boards, El Granada Beach is a good starting point for long walks. Trekking south will take you on an approximately four-mile journey to Half Moon Bay on uninterrupted sandy beaches. For the beach walker, this is a pleasant and invigorating ocean-side hike. Free parking is available in an unpaved parking lot. When this fills, beach goers park along both sides of Highway 1, creating a bottleneck. Beware as people dart across the highway. Restrooms and RV camping is allowed at the north end of the beach in the Harbor District's RV Park. The beach is located just south of the breakwater in El Granada. SEE: Sleeping chapter for additional information.

Quarry Park

Quarry Park is a passive recreational park good for hiking, mountain biking, and horse back riding. The park currently has about 2 ½ miles of trails up the hillside and by the old quarry. A children's play area is located at the entrance to the park beside a horse corral, that shares the property. The original quarry was commissioned by the Ocean Shore Railroad Company to help build the town of El Granada. During World War II, materials from the quarry were used to construct the Half Moon Bay Airport. A kiosk located near the play area gives additional information. Located at the corner of Columbus Avenue and Santa Maria in El Granada.

James V. Fitzgerald Marine Reserve

Walk on the tidepool rocks and discover starfish, crabs, and other shore-based sea life at a minus tide. The Fitzgerald Marine Reserve is one of the best places in California to view tidepools. You can explore three miles of beach and rock inhabited by an abundance of marine life. At low tide over 200 species can be examined "up close and personal." Tide information appears in the daily San Francisco Chronicle and Examiner. In addition, you can pick up tide charts at fish or bait shops on the coast. The marine life is protected and may not be removed. Abalone fishing is prohibited.

Hike on the bluffs overlooking the Reserve and view rocky coves, symmetric patterns of rolling waves, and wind-swept cypress trees guarding the landscape. To miss the Fitzgerald Marine Reserve is to miss the essence of the Coastside. The Reserve has a paved parking lot, restrooms, an interpretive center, and picnic tables. Docent-guided tours are available if reserved in advance. Take California Avenue, off Highway 1 to North Lake Street in Moss Beach. 728-3584. Website: http://bonita.mbnms.nos.noaa.gov/visitor/access/fitz.html. SEE: Sporting chapter for additional information.

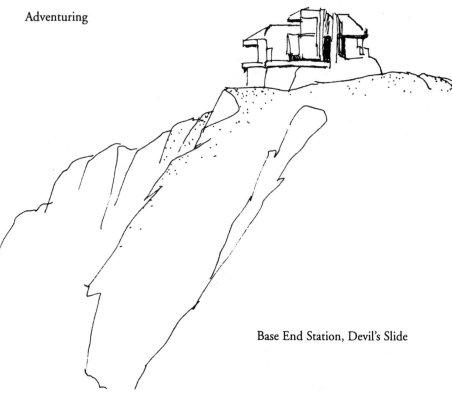

Base End Station, Devil's Slide

Montara State Beach

Don't miss this beautiful, lengthy expanse of sandy beach edged by guarding rocky cliffs. Surfing, surf fishing, kite flying, and beach walking are all enjoyed at this beach, but it is a hazardous surf for swimming, so be alert. Parking is about three-fourths miles north of the Chart House Restaurant. Stairway to the beach. An additional parking lot just south of the Chart House has portable restrooms. Highway 1 and 2nd Street, Montara. Website: www.cal-parks.ca.gov.

Montara Mountain/McNee Ranch State Park

A spectacular view of San Francisco Bay awaits the energetic hiker and mountain biker. Follow the trail just beyond the entry gate and enjoy Martini Creek as it cuts through Montara Mountain, home to many California native birds and mammals, including two endangered species, the peregrine falcon and the San Bruno elfin butterfly. Just to the north of the creek is McNee Ranch where you'll find additional trails. Montara Mountain and McNee Ranch are a part of Montara State Beach. Parking is available at the beach lots. The entry is east of Highway 1 across from the north end of Montara State Beach. 726-8819. Website: www:cardiffgiant.com/ ptmcn.html. SEE: Sporting chapter for more information

Gray Whale Cove State Beach

A more dramatic and beautiful beach than Gray Whale Cove would be very hard to find. The cove, the expanse of sand, and the protective cliffs will make you linger. Follow the path to the clothing-optional beach below the bluffs. A parking lot is on the east side of the highway. Cross the highway with care. There are entrance fees and restrooms on the beach. The beach is open on weekends and some holidays (728-5336). To the north, on the hilltop, you can see the remains of the Base End Station, used for observation during World War II. It isn't hard to imagine enemy submarines lurking nearby. Heed the posted signs and don't attempt to climb to the ruins. The stairway is crumbling and very dangerous. Highway 1 south of Devil's Slide.

SOUTH COAST

Martin's Beach

Looking for that long lost beach cove with mythical pirates and treasure? This small coastal village enclave is the beach for you. Sandy beaches line a secluded cove; a gathering of cabins hug the cliffs leading down to the beach. There is an entrance fee, parking lot, restrooms, picnic tables, and fishing net rentals. Located off Highway 1, six miles south of Half Moon Bay. 712-8020.

San Gregorio Private Beach

This beach is known primarily as a nude beach. Open on weekends. Entrance fee. Located off Highway 1, one-forth mile north of San Gregorio Road.

San Gregorio State Beach

With its expanse of sand for hiking, volleyball, surf fishing (rockfish and perch), picnicking, and sun bathing, San Gregorio is an excellent beach for families or individuals. Because of the undertow, it is not for swimming. The lagoon, where San Gregorio Creek enters the ocean, offers you an inviting, safe, and slightly warmer swimming hole. A California Historical Landmark marks the spot where Spanish explorer Gasper de Portolá and his men camped in 1769 on their way north. Entrance fee, parking lots, restrooms, grass area, picnic tables, and fire pits. Highway l, 10 ½ miles south of Half Moon Bay. 726-6238.

Pomponio State Beach

Classic palisades are the back drop for this driftwood strewn beach. You will find this a narrower beach than San Gregorio, but it offers most of the same amenities—parking, restrooms, picnic tables, and fire pits. Surf fishing and beach combing on the sandy beach, and wildflowers along the bluffs in the spring are an attraction for hikers. Entrance fees. Highway l, twelve miles south of Half Moon Bay.

Pescadero State Beach

There is a little bit of everything at Pescadero Beach—two miles of sandy beaches, dunes, tidepools, and rocky promontories; this is a good all purpose beach. Mussels abound (check with the Department of Fish and Game, (916) 653-7664 for quarantine dates) and occasionally seals and sea lions can be seen sunning themselves on rocks just off shore. Ample parking is available. The middle lot offers restrooms, picnic tables, and barbecue pits. Located off Highway 1 opposite Pescadero Road, 14 ½ miles south of Half Moon Bay. 879-2170. Website: www.cal-parks.ca.gov.

Pescadero Marsh Natural Reserve

Enjoy a different piece of Coastside nature by lacing up your walking shoes and heading for the Pescadero Marsh, one of the largest and most important marshes in California. This wildlife sanctuary is a favorite of birdwatchers and other animal lovers. The Marsh contains a wide variety of birds, mammals, amphibians, and plants. Hiking trails take you on a winding journey through over 500 acres of marshlands. Early spring and fall are the optimum times for bird watching at the Marsh.

Pebble Beach, south of Pescadero

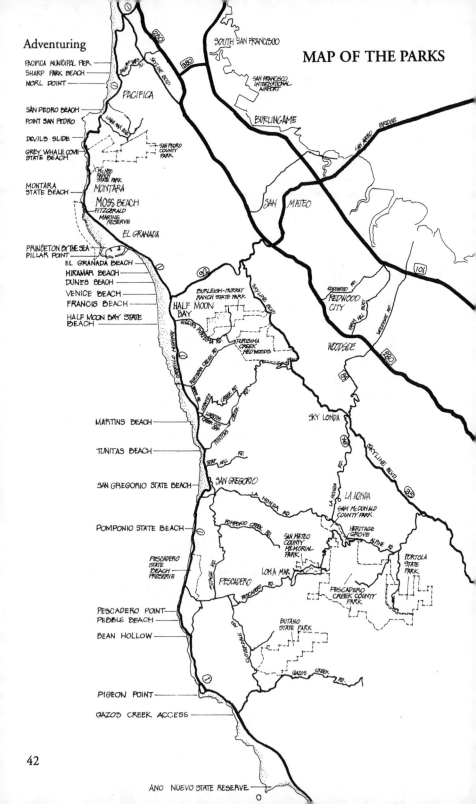

MAP OF THE PARKS

Adventuring

PACIFICA MUNICIPAL PIER
SHARP PARK BEACH
MORI POINT

SAN PEDRO BEACH
POINT SAN PEDRO

DEVILS SLIDE
GREY WHALE COVE
STATE BEACH

MONTARA
STATE BEACH

PRINCETON BY THE SEA
PILLAR POINT
EL GRANADA BEACH
MIRAMAR BEACH
DUNES BEACH
VENICE BEACH
FRANCIS BEACH
HALF MOON BAY STATE
BEACH

MARTINS BEACH

TUNITAS BEACH

SAN GREGORIO STATE BEACH

POMPONIO STATE BEACH

PESCADERO POINT
PEBBLE BEACH

BEAN HOLLOW

PIGEON POINT

GAZOS CREEK ACCESS

ANO NUEVO STATE RESERVE

SOUTH SAN FRANCISCO
SAN FRANCISCO INTERNATIONAL AIRPORT
BURLINGAME
SAN MATEO BRIDGE
PACIFICA
SAN PEDRO COUNTY PARK
MCNEE RANCH STATE PARK
MONTARA
MOSS BEACH
FITZGERALD MARINE RESERVE
EL GRANADA
SAN MATEO
REDWOOD CITY
WOODSIDE
HALF MOON BAY
BURLEIGH-MURRAY RANCH STATE PARK
PURISIMA CREEK REDWOODS
SKY LONDA
SAN GREGORIO
LA HONDA
SAM McDONALD COUNTY PARK
HERITAGE GROVE
PESCADERO STATE BEACH PRESERVE
PESCADERO
SAN MATEO COUNTY MEMORIAL PARK
PORTOLA STATE PARK
LOMA MAR
PESCADERO CREEK COUNTY PARK
BUTANO STATE PARK

42

No pets allowed. Docent-led tours are given on Saturdays at 10:30 a.m. and Sundays at 1 p.m. Meet in the middle Pescadero Beach Parking lot across Highway 1. Pescadero Marsh abuts Highway 1 at Pescadero Road. For information on the docent-led Marsh walks call 879-2170.

Pebble Beach/Bean Hollow State Beach

This attractive, small beach cove is covered with smooth, small, beautifully polished stones. Admire but don't remove them; it is illegal. You'll find this a good place to view the spring wildflowers native to the area and also to do a bit of tidepooling. Stroll the self-guided nature trail to Bean Hollow State Beach, a two-mile roundtrip hike along the bluffs, to see some of California's most spectacular rock and surf scenery. Parking is free and restrooms are available. Located seventeen miles south of Half Moon Bay. 879-2170. SEE: Sporting chapter for additional information.

Butano State Park

Prefer forests to beaches? You'll want to try this 3200 acre park full of redwoods, ferns, and a variety of wildlife. Silver salmon and steelhead trout swim in Butano Creek. Hike the trails with their scenic views, one overlooking Año Nuevo Island. If you camp, there are twenty developed campsites and eighteen walk-in sites, wheelchair-accessible restrooms, fifteen-miles of hiking, picnicking, and fishing. No showers. Informative guided nature walks and weekend campfire programs during summer capture the attention of children and adults. Turn east on Pescadero Road and right on Cloverdale Road for almost five miles. Reservations: (800) 444-7275 or 879-2040. Websites: www.park-net.com and www.cal-parks.ca.gov. SEE: Sleeping chapter for additional information.

Sam McDonald Park

Pescadero Creek County Park
This impressively large county park holds a variety of outdoor finds for recreation lovers of all ages. Pescadero Creek County Park is a group of contiguous parks with continuous trails: San Mateo Memorial County Park, Sam McDonald Park, Pescadero Creek Park, and Heritage Grove Redwood Preserve. Together they spread over 7400 acres of coastal mountains with towering redwood forests, mountain streams, lush fern grottos, and rolling grasslands. A network of hiking and equestrian trails wind through the park. The Pomponio Trail passes through the entire length of the park. Pescadero Creek, which flows year round, is a major steelhead spawning stream. Pescadero Creek Park is located ten miles east of Highway 1 on Pescadero Road. Reservations for the Pescadero Creek County Park System: 363-4021.

San Mateo Memorial County Park
Memorial Park is known for its stands of old growth redwoods, and its people provisions with over 100 campsites for families, picnic facilities, a visitor center, camp store, a creek swimming area, campfire programs, group areas, and trails. This park is

one of the most popular coastal parks. First come-first served camping for families; reservations are required for all youth groups. Call 879-0212 to check on campsite availability. The park is located 9 ½ miles east of Highway 1 on Pescadero Road. SEE: Sleeping chapter for additional information.

Sam McDonald Park

This 870 acre park has, as a centerpiece, groves of old growth redwoods for reflective viewing, but the park also offers beautiful rolling grassland, open ridges, and Pacific Ocean vistas. Hiking trails abound. Camping is available for youth and horse camps only. Reservations are required. A hikers' hut run by the Sierra Club can be rented by the night; call 494-9901 for reservations. The hikers' hut is located 1 ¾ miles from the parking lot. Sam McDonald Park is located 13 ½ miles east of Highway 1 on Pescadero Road. Take Highway 84. Just south of La Honda turn at the three-way intersection on to Pescadero Road. SEE: Sleeping chapter for additional information.

Heritage Grove Redwood Preserve

Heritage Grove is a magnificent old-growth redwood forest connected to other parts of the Pescadero Creek Park by a network of trails. Redwood trees in this park are upwards of fifteen feet in diameter and some over 1000 years old. Many trees still wear the paint marking them to be felled by loggers. Fortunately, the grove was saved and became a county park in 1974. Go east on Highway 84 (La Honda Road). Take Pescadero Road to Alpine Road and go one mile south. A small parking lot will be on your right.

Portola Redwoods State Park

Like the other San Mateo County Parks, Portola State Park has redwood forests and many miles of hiking trails for the hearty hiker and nature lover. Fifty-two overnight campsites are available as are three hike-in group camp areas. Portola State Park is located 6 ½ miles west of Highway 35. Turn off of Alpine Road on to Portola State Park Road. 948-9098. Website: www.park-net.com. SEE: Sleeping chapter for additional information.

Pigeon Point Lighthouse

SEE: Seeing and Sleeping chapters for information on the Lighthouse.

Gazos Creek Coastal Access

Prefer grassy dunes and a rarely crowded beach? Try Gazos. This is a popular fishing location for both surf fishing on the beach and stream fishing on Gazos Creek. Rainbow trout, silver salmon, and steelhead trout are commonly caught. Parking lot and restrooms. Highway 1, north of Gazos Creek Road, south of Pigeon Point.

Cascade Ranch State Park

Controversy has surrounded the Cascade Ranch project for years; however, the California Department of Parks and Recreation, with help from environmental groups, has acquired 3000 acres earmarked to become Cascade Ranch State Park. Eventually, Cascade Ranch State Park will offer miles of hiking trails interconnecting with Big Basin State Park, Gazos Creek, and Año Nuevo. Located off Highway 1, one mile north of Año Nuevo State Reserve.

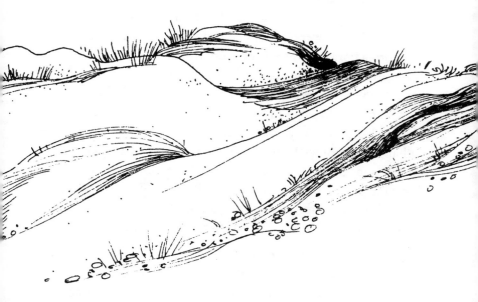

Waddell Creek Beach

Windsurfing, surfing, and miles of sandy beach distinguish Waddell Beach, just south of the San Mateo County line. Waddell bluffs, a natural erosion of rock material on the east side of Highway 1, has a Grand Canyon cliff-side appearance. The talus material, which makes up the body of the crumbly rock, erodes easily in the winter. The debris is taken across the road and deposited on the beach, where the waves provide nature's natural breakdown of deposits.

Rancho del Oso

On the east side of Highway 1, across from Waddell Creek, tucked in the Waddell Valley, is a tiny nature and history center open on Saturdays and Sundays from 12 noon to 4 p.m. There is a one-mile, self-guided interpretive trail; or, for the more ambitious, there is a seven-mile Skyline to ocean trail through redwoods and mixed forest.

Año Nuevo State Reserve

Seeing the elephant seals and their habitat at Año Nuevo should be at the top of every visitor's list. You'll wind through native California flora on a three-mile roundtrip hike over sand dunes and through kelp beds to the breeding grounds of this awkward 6000 pound sea and land mammal. During the breeding season, mid-December to April, reservations are a must for the docent-led tours. As you approach, the first notice of the elephant seals comes from the trumpeting males engaged in mostly mock battles. This group has been culled out of the breeding process by natural selection. Before looking twice you are within several feet of the females and young cubs. They are within reach, but, of course, no touching is allowed.

From April to November the elephant seals are in their molting and haul-out season and they are not as prevalent nor as active. No reservations are required during this time, but permits must be obtained from the Reserve entrance.

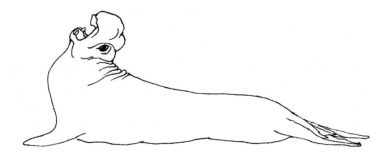

No matter when you go to Año Nuevo, it is an impressive 4000 acre park to visit. The dunes are important scientifically and represent one of the few remaining active dune areas on the California coast. Año Nuevo Reserve, both the island and the mainland, are also home to sea lions and a wide variety of native plants and animals. Besides the dunes, wide sandy beaches enhance the area. Many of the trails are wheelchair accessible. No pets are allowed. Restrooms are available. The parking lot and visitors center are located on New Year's Creek Road off Highway 1, twenty-seven miles south of Half Moon Bay. For reservations during the breeding season, call no more than fifty-six days in advance: (800) 444-4445. The cost of the docent-led tours is $4 per person; there is a $5 per vehicle parking fee. For recorded information call: 879-0227. San Mateo Transit (SamTrans) offers roundtrip fare and guided walk for $12 per person; for Samtrans reservations call 508-6441. Website: www.anonuevo.org.

Greyhound Rock Fishing Access

Just off Highway 1 and south of the county line is Greyhound Rock, a popular fishing area, which is fronted by a large paved parking lot. This public fishing access was developed by the Wildlife Conservation Board and the Department of Fish and Game. Picnic tables are available for excellent panoramic views of the ocean. Portable restrooms are present.

PACIFICA

Rockaway Beach

Rockaway Beach is Pacifica's motel and tourist restaurant center. Surfers and surf fishermen use this beach, but for most people viewing the adjacent rocks and the ocean is the best activity. West of Highway 1, at Rockaway Beach Avenue.

Pedro Point Headlands

Recently purchased by the Pacifica Land Trust, the headlands are now open to the public for hiking. The trails are steep, rough and eroded, but the profusion of wildflowers, and the dramatic views of the Pacific Ocean overlooking Shelter Cove, are worth the climb. Parking is very limited. The trail head is marked by a sign off Highway 1 between Devil's Slide and Pacifica, just south of Linda Mar. A few cars can park on the left side of the road near the trail head; additional parking is on the right hand side north of the trail head.

Pacifica State Beach

A very popular beach on sunny days, this expansive sandy beach is a magnet for the Pacifica beach goer. Surfing is popular for the adept, and digging for littleneck clams and cockles is available to anyone with patience, a shovel, and a bucket. The beach is hazardous for swimming due to currents and rip tides. Paved parking lot, wheelchair-accessible restrooms, outdoor showers, and a boat ramp. Highway 1 between Crespi Drive and Linda Mar Blvd. Website: www.cal-parks.ca.gov.

San Pedro Valley County Park

This is a surprise find of a sunny 1150 acre nature park tucked away from the often foggy beaches of Pacifica. Hiking trails take you through wooded areas that are home to many California native species of plants and animals including the San Francisco garter snake. The wildflowers can be magnificent in the spring. Wheelchair-accessible restrooms and self-guided nature trails are available. There is an interpretive center, picnic tables, and barbecue pits. Open 8 a.m. to dusk. Off Highway 1, take Linda Mar Blvd that dead ends at Oddstad Blvd. Turn right into the park. 355-8289. SEE: Sporting chapter for additional information.

Sweeney Ridge

There are few views as grand as those of San Francisco Bay, with the sweep of water and coastal mountains edging to the shore. Scientists tell us that it is not a bay at all but rather an estuary. This scientific nicety may not occupy your thoughts as you view one of the natural wonders of Northern California from Sweeney Ridge. Such thoughts certainly did not concern Captain Don Gaspar de Portolá as his expedition of Spanish explorers first set sight on San Francisco Bay from this same ridge in 1769.

Sweeney Ridge Skyline Preserve and San Francisco Bay Discovery Site is a part of the Golden Gate National Recreational Area. The trail to the top of Sweeney Ridge is steep, but worth your while on a clear day. Spring and fall are the best times of the year for a climb. Wildflowers and wildlife abound at certain times during the year. Ranger-led walks are conducted quarterly and focus on varying appropriate topics. Call (415) 239-2366 for additional information on the free walks.

For access to the discovery site from Pacifica, begin at the upper parking lot of the Shelldance Nursery. The trail head for this 2 ¼ mile walk is marked with a brown and yellow Golden Gate National Recreational Area sign. The nursery is located at 2000 Cabrillo Highway, on the east side of the road, north of Vallemar in Pacifica.

Two other access points begin in San Bruno. The shortest trail, 1 8/10 miles to the Discovery Site, begins off Sneath Lane. Take Skyline Blvd in San Bruno, turn west on Sneath Lane to the parking lot marked Sweeney Ridge Gate. Another access point in San Bruno begins at Skyline College. Take Highway 35, turn west on College Drive, and go to the south side of Skyline College to Parking Lot #2 for the trail head. This trail is two miles to the Discovery Site. (415) 556-8371. Website: www.ci.pacifica.ca.us/natural.

Milagra Ridge Park

This 232 acre park for hiking and biking is a part of the Golden Gate National Recreation Area. Trails are easy and relatively flat and are readily accessible to the nearby parking lot. On a clear day, this is a good place to bring out of town visitors for a short scenic walk to show off the Pacific Ocean stretching from Pacifica to Marin County. In the spring, admire the wildflowers and butterflies, including the rare Mission Blue and San Bruno Elfin butterflies. Turn east on Sharp Park Blvd off of Highway 1 in Pacifica. Turn left at College Drive which dead ends at the parking lot and trail head. 556-8371. Website: www.ci.pacifica.ca.us/natural.

Pacifica Municipal Pier

SEE: Seeing chapter for information on the pier.

Frontierland Park

Frontierland Park is an extensive local park with varied play equipment for children, a par course, forest, open space, and a barbecue picnic area. Group picnic sites are available. Children will be especially pleased with this spot. Restrooms and parking lots. Take Linda Mar Blvd until it ends, then left on Oddstad and right on Yosemite Drive in Pacifica. Reservations for the group sites: 363-4021.

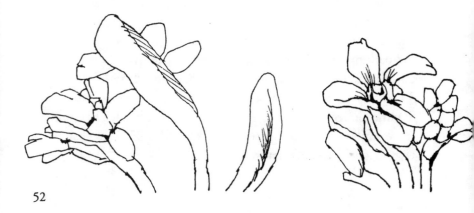

NATURING

Wildflowers

Wildflower displays on the coastside can be subtle with hues of light mauve from wild radish, tinges of yellow yarrow and an occasional red-orange paint brush in among the gray green sea grasses and coastal shrubs covering the coastal range. But, sometimes coastal wildflowers can be outrageous in their display: patches of tiny wild iris, hillsides of California poppies, and fields of bright yellow wild mustard. The assortment, timing and intensity depends on the winter rains and the warm spring sunshine. Generally, the best places to find coastal wildflowers are:

Montara Mountain at McNee Ranch State Park, especially the trail to Gray Whale Cove. Check with Go Native Nursery (728-0728) for organized wildflower hikes on Montara Mountain in the spring.

Coastside Trail between Mirada Avenue in Miramar and Kelly Avenue in Half Moon Bay.

The bluff trail between Pebble Beach and Bean Hollow State Beach, south of Pescadero Road.

Butano State Park. Nature walks are led every Saturday and Sunday at 2 p.m. during the summer. 879-2040.

San Pedro Valley Park, especially the Hazelnut Trail. Call 355-8289 for additional information.

Sweeney Ridge. Ranger-led walks are conducted quarterly. Call to make reservations and to find out the topic of each walk: (415) 239-2366.

Birds and Butterflies

Hundreds of species of birds, both natives and migratory, fly the coastal region: great blue herons, snowy egrets, red winged black birds, brown pelicans, and a variety of gulls to name a few. Birding lists are available from the Half Moon Bay Chamber of Commerce. The best places for bird watching are:

Pillar Point Wetlands and Western Shoreline Access in Princeton-by-the-Sea. Take the trail to the left of the radar station to Pillar Point Reef for additional birding.

Pescadero Marsh Natural Preserve. Free docent-led walks are available on Saturdays at 10:30 a.m. and Sundays at 1 p.m. Call 879-2170 for additional information.

Pigeon Point, north of the Pigeon Point Lighthouse is a favorite South Coast spot to observe sea birds.

Año Nuevo Reserve, thirty-five miles south of Half Moon Bay.

Yerba Buena Nursery, off Highway 35, across from the Thomas Fogarty Winery.

Milagra Ridge, see Mission Blue and San Bruno Elfin butterflies from April to June, in Pacifica.

Sharp Park Golf Course freshwater marsh, south of Sharp Park Beach, Pacifica.

Sweeney Ridge in Pacifica.

Tidepooling

Finding a star fish or sand crab in its tidepool home is a thrilling experience for children and adults alike. But to appreciate tidepooling at its best, go during minus tides. Pick up tide charts at most fishing or bait shops on the coast. Daily tide information appears on the weather page of the San Francisco Chronicle and Examiner. Tidepooling can best be enjoyed at:

James V. Fitzgerald Marine Reserve

Pebble Beach/Bean Hollow State Beach

Año Nuevo State Reserve

Elephant Seals and Whales

Año Nuevo is home to a large colony of elephant seals, one of the few places in the world to see these unique creatures. Año Nuevo is also a very good place to watch birds, whales and other wildlife. Access to the reserve area is by reservations only during the breeding season from mid-December to April. Call 879-0227 for information and (800) 444-4445 for reservations.

Gray whales may be seen migrating to their winter calving and breeding grounds in Baja California (November to February) and throughout spring (March and April) as they return to summer feeding in the Arctic. You know you have seen a whale by the spout of water, up to ten feet in the air, exhaled by the whales before they dive. Whales will resurface again a few minutes later and then about 1000 feet further along the coast.

For best places to see whales from the shoreline try:

The Pacifica Municipal Pier

Montara Mountain

The Coastside Trail

Francis Beach, Half Moon Bay State Beach

Davenport Overlook

Whale watching trips by boat give the spectator a whole new sense of awe and amazement of the size and power of these ocean-bound mammals. You can depart from Pillar Point Harbor during the whale runs:

Captain John's (728-3377) and Huck Finn's (726-7133) sportfishing boats. Trips usually are on weekends only at 8 a.m., 11 a.m., and 2 p.m., and last for about two hours.

The Oceanic Society leads whale watching trips with a naturalist, also departing from Pillar Point Harbor, every weekend from the end of December through April. (415) 441-1106.

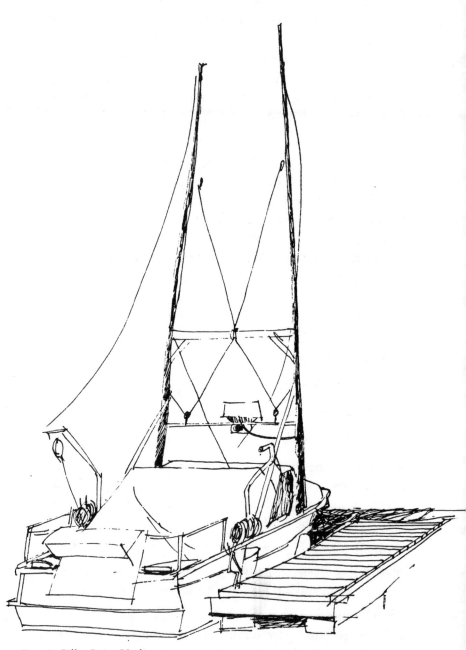

Boat in Pillar Point Harbor

5

SPORTING

Cycle over the coastal bluffs, bareback ride through the surf, fish for steelhead in the mountain streams; scuba dive, swim, and golf. There are many sporting possibilities on the Coastside.

The sports activities are listed in alphabetical order. For some entries, such as biking and hiking, you will find suggested itineraries. These are starting points for your further explorations.

Have fun!

ARCHERY

For archery enthusiasts, especially those who wish to do their shooting on target trails, the **San Francisco Archery Range** offers two target practice paths in heavily wooded and steep terrain, with twenty-eight targets each. There is also a kid's practice range. The range is open to the public daily from sunrise to sunset. It is located in Pacifica off Lundy Way. Take the Sharp Park exit off Highway 1, turn right, and follow the signs to the archery range. 355-9947.

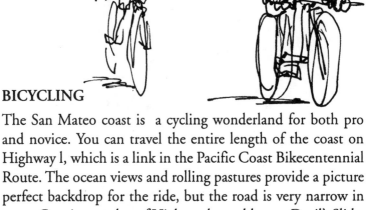

BICYCLING

The San Mateo coast is a cycling wonderland for both pro and novice. You can travel the entire length of the coast on Highway 1, which is a link in the Pacific Coast Bikecentennial Route. The ocean views and rolling pastures provide a picture perfect backdrop for the ride, but the road is very narrow in spots. Certain stretches of Highway 1, notably over Devil's Slide, is only for the experienced. For hostel stayers, the distance from Montara Lighthouse Youth Hostel to Pigeon Point Lighthouse Youth Hostel is thirty miles.

Half Moon Bay Bike Rental, 648 Kelly Ave., #4, in downtown Half Moon Bay provides rentals. All types of bikes are available for both casual riders and families. Open weekends, 10 a.m. to 7 p.m. Reasonable rates. Website: Http://smart.sbay.com/hmb-bikes. 712-4499

Best Bike Rides:
1. The Coastside Trail: *Six-miles round trip; easy, level trail.*
This scenic biking and hiking trail stretches from Pillar Point
Harbor in Princeton to Redondo Beach, south of Half Moon
Bay along the ocean bluffs. There is a short stretch at Surfer's
Beach in El Granada, where the bike path is incomplete and
riders must go on Highway 1. Or, start the trail at the end of
Mirada Road in Miramar Beach. The Coastside Trail mean-
ders past sand dunes, through fields of wild flowers and groves
of Monterey pines and eucalyptus, and awards you with spec-
tacular ocean vistas. Rabbits and many species of birds make
this trail their home. Occasionally gray whale are spotted off
shore. Join the trail at any one of several access points along
Highway 1, between Pillar Point Harbor and Half Moon Bay:
Roosevelt Beach, Dunes Beach, Venice Beach, or Francis Beach.

2. Burleigh Murray State Park: *about seven-miles round trip:
easy, level trail.* Begin on Main Street in Half Moon Bay cycling south to Highway 1. Just before reaching Highway 1,
turn left on Higgins Purisima Road. The historic James
Johnston House in on your right. Continue for about 1½
miles through farm land and rolling California countryside to
the Burleigh Murray State Park parking lot on your left. The
trail through the park to the old dairy buildings is about two
miles of flat, well-graded road. Veer to the left at the ranger's
house to see the bank barn.

3. Pillar Point Harbor to Fitzgerald Marine Reserve: *Six-miles
round trip; easy, level trail.* Cycling is a pleasure throughout the
Pillar Point Harbor area. Cycle to Capistrano Road in front of
Pillar Point Harbor. Turn west on Prospect, right on Broad-
way, and follow the bike trail signs to Airport Road. Ride to
the end of Airport Road, turn right on Cypress and rejoin
Highway 1. It is just a short distance north on Highway 1 to
California Street, turn left and continue to the Fitzgerald Marine Reserve.

4. Sunshine Valley Road, Montara to Moss Beach: *four-miles round trip; moderately difficult.* This is a ride through pastoral California scenery on a somewhat hilly, narrow, pleasant, winding road past a number of horse ranches. Begin at Main Street, Montara, turn right on 4th Street through several blocks of residential area. Turn right on George Street, which becomes Sunshine Valley Road. The route is a semi-circular journey that ends in Moss Beach at Etheldore Street; go right on Highway 1 and continue back to Montara.

5. South Coast trips: There is a wide variety of bicycling possibilities in the South Coast area. A glance at a good map will help you choose the many prospects and combinations. Most of the trips listed are on narrow, steep roads. These can be rewarding for the well-equipped athlete but difficult for the novice. For example: (1) Stage Road, connecting San Gregorio with Pescadero; (2) Gazos Creek Road, to Cloverdale Road past Butano State Park and back to Pescadero; (3) Tunitas Creek Road, from the coast to the mountains at Skyline; (4) Pescadero Road, from the coast, through the town of Pescadero and on to San Mateo County Memorial Park; (5) La Honda Road, from the coast to the mountains. The combinations are virtually endless for the enterprising cyclist.

6. From the Pacifica Pier to Sharp Park Golf Course: *four-miles round trip; easy, level trail.* For an easy, short, but beautiful bike ride, start at the northern end of Beach Blvd in Pacifica. Cycle along the promenade past the Pacifica Pier. Keep going south in back of the Sharp Park Golf Course. The trail is on top of a berm, with the ocean on one side and the golf course marsh area on the other. This is also an excellent walking trail, especially popular with dog walkers. Mountain bikers and energetic hikers can continue on one of several trails into the hills over Mori Point.

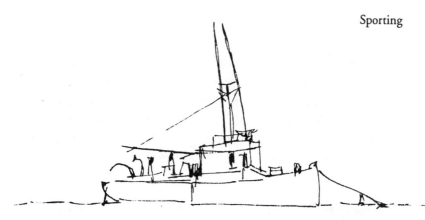

BOATING

What is an ocean without boats? And boats and boating opportunities are plentiful along the San Mateo coast. The Pillar Point Harbor has berths for 250 commercial fishing vessels and 150 pleasure boats. There are twenty-four hour launch ramps, dinghy hoist, public restrooms, fuel dock, public pier for fishing, and recreational vehicle parking lot. And even if you are not a boating enthusiast, just viewing the many yachts and commercial boats is an enjoyable activity. Call the Harbor Master at 726-4382 for specific boating information. SEE: Adventuring Chapter for additional information.

Sailing

Sail boats can anchor in the Pillar Point Harbor between the inner and outer breakwater. Call the Harbor Master at 726-4382 for exact mooring location. The Half Moon Bay Yacht Club facilities can be used by members of other yacht clubs. 728-2120.

Canoeing and Kayaking

California Canoe and Kayak holds classes, sponsors outings, and rents canoes and kayaks at Pillar Point Harbor. Sea Kayak classes are held for all skill levels. Kayaking trips are sponsored throughout the year. Open weekends from 9 a.m. to 5 p.m.; 214 Princeton Avenue. 728-1803. Call 800-366-9804 for advanced reservations. Website: www.calkayak.com.

BOWLING

Sea Bowl is a newly remodeled state of the art, full-service bowling facility with panoramic views of the Pacific Ocean. There is also a video arcade, billiard room, full-service pro shop, and bar and grill. It is open daily from 11 a.m. to midnight. 4625 Coast Highway, Pacifica. 738-8190.

FISHING

Fishing is the leading coastside sporting activity with many opportunities for different styles of fishing and different types of fish. Permitted without a license on any man-made structure such as a pier or breakwater. Licenses are required for fishing on boats and off the beach. For fishing regulations call the local State Department of Fish and Game at 688-6340 or the Sacramento headquarter office at 916-653-7664. Website: www.dfg.ca.gov.

Pier Fishing
Johnson Pier on Pillar Point Harbor in Princeton: Fish for salmon, rockfish, halibut, and crab on this public pier. Rod and reel rentals are available. Restrooms and twenty-four hour recreational vehicle parking lot are on site. The Pier is located

west of Highway 1 on Capistrano Road in Princeton. SEE: Boating, this chapter, for information on launches, and Deep Sea Fishing for information on party boats. SEE: The Seeing Chapter for additional information on the Harbor.

Pacifica Municipal Pier on Sharp Park Beach in Pacifica: The concrete pier extends over 1000 feet into the ocean. The fishing is good for salmon, striped bass, crab, sole, king fish, flounder, perch, sand dabs, and halibut. No license is required. Restrooms, lights for night fishing, concessions for food and drinks, rental equipment, and bait are available. There is good whale watching potential and excellent views of Pedro Point. Beach Blvd at Santa Rosa Avenue in Pacifica. 355-0690. SEE: The Seeing Chapter for additional information on the pier.

Surf Fishing

Surf fishing, mostly for rockfish and perch, is good all along the coast from Pacifica south to Año Nuevo. One day fishing licenses are available at Pacifica Municipal Pier and Johnson Pier at Pillar Point Harbor. Surf smelt fishing is best at Martin's Beach, south of Half Moon Bay, from April to November. Net rentals are available.

Deep Sea Fishing

For those who prefer deep sea fishing, party boats leave daily from Pillar Point Harbor in Princeton. Salmon, rockfish, and crab are caught offshore. One day licenses and rod and reel rentals are available for sports boat fishing. Several companies provide all day deep sea fishing trips; most are located on Johnson Pier in Pillar Point Harbor: **Captain John's Fishing Trips**, 728-3377; **Huck Finn Fishing Trips**, 726-7133. **Wild Wave Excursions**, 712-9453; and **Reel Sport**, 712-1740. Open daily, weather permitting.

Marine Warehouse in Princeton furnishes salt water fishing equipment and supplies and also has listings for additional private charter fishing boats. 151 Howard Avenue in Princeton.

728-7725. The fishing hotline is 728-0627; call to get the latest weather and fishing reports. Or, view the latest Half Moon Bay fishing report on the web: http://usafishing.com/halfmoon.html. Other places to pick up fishing supplies and tips on where the fish are biting, are **Hilltop Grocery and Fishing Supplies,** 251 Highway 92, on the left as you enter Half Moon Bay; the piers, in Pacifica and Pillar Point Harbor; and Martin's Beach, south of Half Moon Bay.

For sports fishing in your own boat, six launch ramps are available at Pillar Point Harbor. Small dock facilities can also be found at San Pedro Beach in Pacifica where king salmon, crab, and rock fishing are good. Offshore fishing at Año Nuevo on the South Coast is excellent.

Stream Fishing

If you are a stream fisherman the coastal streams provide challenging conditions for catching salmon and steelhead. At the right time of the year steelhead trout and silver salmon migrate upstream for spawning in a number of locations. Pescadero Creek, which flows into the ocean at Pescadero State Beach, is an ideal fishing location. Gazos Creek, a little further south along Highway 1, is stocked with rainbow trout during the summer; silver salmon and steelhead trout spawn upstream.

Trout Farms

Fish the easy way at the **Lintt Trout Farm** by catching rainbow trout in a well-stocked small pond. No license is required.

Pole rentals available. Open daily from 10 a.m. to 4 p.m. 11751 Highway 92, Half Moon Bay. 726-0845.

Abalone Fishing

As of January 1, 1998, it is illegal to take abalone from the ocean off the San Mateo County coast and the Farallon Islands.

Mussel Gathering

Mussel gathering has an imposed limit of ten pounds (in the shell) at any one time. Mussels can contain a deadly toxin from the late spring to early fall months. Check with the California Department of Fish and Game at (916)-653-7664 to make sure they are safe before gathering. Pescadero State Beach and other South Coast beaches are best bets for mussel collecting.

GOLF

Half Moon Bay Golf Links has two challenging, championship courses, both offering spectacular ocean views. Some holes are positioned dramatically on the bluffs overlooking the ocean. The newer Ocean Course is a 6,732-yard, par-72 golf course. Green fees are $115 on weekdays and $135 on weekends, including the mandatory cart. The Links Course is a 7,131-yard, par-75 course. The green fees are $95 on weekdays and $115

on weekends. Twilight rates are available for both courses. Call for reservations on either course: 726-4438. **Caddy's Restaurant** is in the club house and opens daily for breakfast, lunch, and dinner. South of Half Moon Bay on Highway 1, turn right on Miramontes Point Road.

Sharp Park Golf Course is a popular eighteen hole, 6,386-yard, par-72 municipal course. The course is, to coin a phrase, landscaped sharply and includes many impressive ocean views. Players refer to the course as a poor man's Pebble Beach. The early California-style designed club house features a full service bar and restaurant open daily from 6 a.m. to 10 p.m. Green fees are $23 on weekdays and $27 weekends. Located on Francisco Blvd in Pacifica. The entry is south of the Sharp Park Road overpass off Highway 1. 359-3380.

HIKING

Don your boots and hike throughout the Coastside. See the Biking Section in this chapter for additional ideas for hikes. Following are a few favorite locales:

1. Purisima Creek Redwoods Open Space: The 2500 acre park has an impressive twenty miles of hiking trails through redwoods and fern-filled creek beds. A wooden map at the entrance to the park shows the various trails. A popular hike, the Whittemore Gulch Trail, takes you to Skyline Blvd for a round trip hike of about six miles. The parking lot for the preserve's coastside entrance is about four miles east of Highway 1, on Higgins Purisima Road. The main entrance is located on Skyline, about 4 ½ miles south of Highway 92. A short, but pretty wheel chair accessible trail through the redwoods begins about 6 ½ miles south of Highway 92 off Skyline. SEE: Adventuring Chapter for additional information.

2. Princeton-by-the-Sea: *One-mile round trip; easy, level trail.* To recreate the feeling of the rum runners, hike around the back side of the Pillar Point Air Force Station in Princeton.

Park your car in the parking lot in front of the Pillar Point Marsh at the base of the Air Force radar station. Walk along the shoreline path, noting the wide variety of birds that migrate to this fresh and salt water marsh. Here are some of the best views of the coastside, including the harbor, with cloud-shrouded mountains in the back ground. As you round the bend, the Pacific Ocean crashes at your feet. If you're lucky you may see a world class surfer paddling out to catch the waves at Mavericks, or, you might see harbor seals sunning themselves on the rocks. For a better view of Mavericks, climb the steep overlook at the end of the trail. From Highway 1, turn on to Capistrano Road in Princeton, and work your way to the parking lot under the Air Force Station hill. SEE: Adventuring Chapter for additional information on Mavericks.

3. Bluffs above the Fitzgerald Marine Reserve: You'll walk under a canopy of cypress trees and see rocky coves and a bird's-eye view of the waves and tidepools below. This is a short walk with magnificent ocean views from the bluffs. At the time of this writing, the bridge at the beginning of this trail is out. Walk a short distance away from the ocean and through the underbrush up to the bluffs. The Fitzgerald Marine Reserve is located off Highway 1 in Moss Beach. Turn west on California Street, to North Lake Blvd.

4. Mavericks lookout walk: From The Moss Beach Distillery to Pillar Point Harbor. This is a beautiful extension to the above hike and adds about three-miles round trip. Begin at the Moss Beach Distillery and walk south along Ocean Blvd. The trail head begins at the end of Ocean Blvd. Walk along the bluffs toward the Air Force Radar Station, through wild flowers over an eroded path. Just beyond the Radar Station, if the waves are up, you will see tiny surfers in the distance. This is Mavericks. Continue on the trail towards Pillar Point Harbor. The road takes you down to the harbor restaurants for an inviting bowl of clam chowder before you return to Moss Beach.

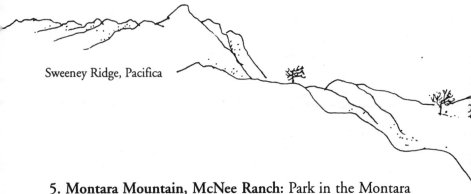

Sweeney Ridge, Pacifica

5. Montara Mountain, McNee Ranch: Park in the Montara State Beach parking lot and walk the short distance across the highway to the entrance of the park. The dirt road leads past the ranger's residence. For beautiful views, stay on the old road that serpentines through Montara Mountain over the saddle between Montara Mountain and San Pedro Mountain, which four miles later ends up in Linda Mar, in Pacifica. This is a steep trail, taking you more than 1000 feet above sea level. Alternately, from the entrance point take the narrower foot path that circles up and around the mountain-side. The views of the ocean are unsurpassed. The trail ends at the Gray Whale Cove parking lot, approximately two miles from the starting point. SEE: Adventuring Chapter for additional information.

6. Pescadero Marsh: Miles of hiking trails wind through this 533 acre wildlife preserve. The marsh is located on the east side of Highway 1 at Pescadero Road. Maps are generally available at the trail entrances, or you can follow the trail markers through the Marsh. SEE: Seeing Chapter for additional information on the Marsh.

7. The Pescadero Creek County Park: Composed of San Mateo Memorial, Sam McDonald, Pescadero CreekCounty Park, and Heritage Grove Redwood Preserve has miles of hiking trails of varying length and difficulty. These wind mostly through redwood forests. The Pomponio Trail passes through the entire

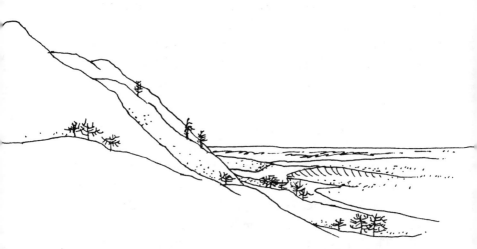

length of the park. Pick up detailed hiking trail maps at one of the ranger stations in the parks. San Mateo Memorial County Park and Sam McDonald Park are located east of Highway 1 on Pescadero Road; Heritage Grove is located off of Highway 84 and Pescadero Road, on Alpine Road. SEE: Adventuring Chapter for additional information.

8. Bluffs from Pebble Beach to Bean Hollow: For an enjoyable and easy two-mile round trip walk past tide pools, a seal rookery, and ocean scapes, walk the bluffs connecting Pebble Beach to Bean Hollow. These beaches are located south of Pescadero off Highway 1. SEE: Adventuring Chapter for additional information.

9. Butano State Park: This 2,200 acre park has over fifteenmiles of hiking trails, one with scenic views of Año Nuevo Island. To reach Butano, go east on Pescadero Road, turn right onto Cloverdale Road for almost five miles. SEE: Adventuring Chapter for additional information.

10. Año Nuevo State Reserve: This is a wonderful walk when the elephant seals are in residence (December to April), however, it can be just as nice when they are not there. During their "off season" you can walk individually at your own pace over the dunes. The approximately three-mile hike provides views of a wide variety of native plants and animals. Año Nuevo is located at New Year's Creek Road off Highway l, thirty- five miles south of Half Moon Bay. SEE: Adventuring Chapter for additional information.

11. Sweeney Ridge: If you want to follow in the footsteps of Portolá, who first saw San Francisco Bay from this vantage point, hike to the top of Sweeney Ridge. But go on a clear day for the best views. The trail head begins at the upper parking lot of the Shelldance Nursery, 2000 Cabrillo Highway, Pacifica. Look for the Golden Gate National Recreation area sign. SEE: The Seeing Chapter for more information.

12. San Pedro Valley Park: A visit to San Pedro, a 1,150 acre park, will reward you with a variety of hikes through the oak studded hillsides. These trails range from a short three-fourths mile hike to Brooks Falls, to the longer trails leading over Montara Mountain. Maps are available at the Ranger Station. 600 Oddstad Blvd, Pacifica. 355-8289. SEE: Adventuring Chapter for additional information.

HORSEBACK RIDING

Feel like Lawrence of Arabia as you gallop over the sand dunes and into the surf. Or you can take the high country rides into the redwood forests and over mountain pastureland. **Sea Horse Ranch** rents horses by the hour for trail rides, beach rides and sunset rides. They are located very near the beach, about one-mile north of Half Moon Bay on Highway 1. Open 8 a.m. to 6 p.m. daily. 726-9903.

SCUBA DIVING

Anderson's Scuba School: Professional, trained instructors give scuba certification courses in a heated, indoor pool. Rentals of scuba and skin diving equipment are by the day or weekend. Open Monday to Friday 12 noon to 7 p.m.; Saturday 10 a.m. to 5 p.m. 541 Oceana Blvd, Pacifica. 355-3050.

SURFING

When the surf is up, the world class surfers migrate to the area north of Pillar Point Harbor, dubbed Mavericks. This is a very dangerous wave and only for experienced surfers. SEE: the Hiking section of this chapter and the Adventuring Chapter, Mavericks section for directions.

The best windsurfing conditions can be found at Waddell Creek Beach, just south of the San Mateo County line in Santa Cruz. It is worth the drive to see the dozens of brightly colored wind sails riding the ocean waves.

Windsurfer

In El Granada many surfers head for the area just south of the breakwater called Surfer's Beach. It is the most popular and visible spot for local surfing. Other, more gentle waves can be found at Francis Beach in Half Moon Bay, at the end of Kelly Avenue. During the summer months, try Año Nuevo Beach. In Pacifica, the best surfing areas can be found at Pedro Point, Pacifica State Beach in Linda Mar, Sharp Park Beach, Pacifica Manor Beach and Rockaway Beach, all off Highway 1. For information on wave swells, temperatures and wind speed, visit the following website: www.HMBSurfCo.com.

Surf Shops

Several surf shops on the coastside can supply boards, wetsuits and all types of surfing apparel. **Coastside Half Moon Bay Surf and Skate Shop** (726-6422) is located at 530 Main Street, Half Moon Bay. **Half Moon Bay Board Shop** (726-1476) is located at 3032 N. Highway 1 and **Cowboy Surf Shop** (726-6968) is at 2830 N. Highway 1, both in Miramar. **Maverick's Surf Shop and Clark Surfboards** is located at 111 Stanford Avenue, Princeton-by-the-Sea. 728-0503.

Sonlight Surf Shop provides rentals and sales of surfboards, boogie boards and sportswear. Call for daily surf conditions. Lessons are given with at least a two-week notice. 575 Crespi Drive, Suite l, Pacifica. 359-0353.

NorCal Surf Shop also rents and sells all surfing equipment. 5460 Highway 1, Pacifica. 738-WAVE.

SWIMMING

Inviting as it may look, swimming in the ocean can be extremely hazardous along the San Mateo coast. The water temperature of approximately 50°F makes it generally too cold for swimming without wet suits. In addition, dangerous rip tides are found just offshore at many of the beaches.

Instead try indoor swimming in a Victorian house converted to a pool and sports club. **Petite Baleen** has a small, indoor pool that offers many amenities. Year round lessons are given Monday through Saturday. The center also provides a workroom, weight room, aerobics and water workouts, spa, and massage room. Pay per visit or buy a pass. 775 Main Street, Half Moon Bay. 726-3676.

Anderson's Swim School is a full service swim school offering private and semi-private swim lessons and safety classes for children in a heated indoor pool. 541 Oceana Blvd, Pacifica. 355-3050.

High School Pools: Two high schools in the area open their doors to drop-in swimmers in the evenings and during the summer months. Call for operating hours and fees. Half Moon Bay High School at 726-4441. Oceana High School in Pacifica at 355-3786.

Pigeon Point Lighthouse

6

SLEEPING

The brisk morning air braces you for a stroll on the beach, the fog horn blows in the distance, and the waves lap onto the shore. A weekend getaway on the coast refreshes both body and soul.

In recent years bed and breakfasts, country inns, and roadside hotels and motels have sprung up like pumpkin blossoms. For the recreationally inclined there are youth hostels in lighthouse settings, hikers' huts in mountain parks, coastside RV parks, and an array of camping spots along the ocean or in mountain parks. There is an overnight spot for everyone.

Sleeping

Half Moon Bay Beach

We have reviewed the accommodations, noting their comfort level, attractiveness, graciousness of proprietors, price, and cleanliness. But, please note that owners, conditions, and prices of accommodations can change rapidly.

Dollar signs ($) represent the per room/per night price range:

$	Inexpensive	Under $100
$$	Moderate	$100 to $150
$$$	Moderately Expensive	$150 to $200
$$$$	Expensive	$200 and up

Most of the hotels, inns, and recreational sites require advanced reservations and many have weekday rates that can be as much as 20% lower than weekend prices. We list the bed and breakfast inns and hotels first, followed by the youth hostels and camping facilities. Geographically, we move from Half Moon Bay, to the Mid-Coast, to the South Coast, and conclude in Pacifica. There are a number of websites devoted to booking rooms on the coastside. Try www.coastside.net/harbormoon/the inns and www.inntraveler.com.

HALF MOON BAY

Mill Rose Inn

Is the ideal bed and breakfast a two-story white cottage with blue trim? Is it surrounded by a white picket fence and a beautiful overflowing garden, always in bloom? If so, you are in luck with the Mill Rose Inn. A profusion of flowers surrounds a secluded back patio area, often the site for small weddings and elegant garden parties. Champagne is served in the private gazebo spa area. Each of the six suites has its own fireplace, bath, outside entrance, and robe for strolling to and from the spa. The decorator wallpaper, bed spreads, and antique furniture are accented with bouquets of flowers. The Mill Rose includes a gourmet breakfast. A minimum of two nights on weekends. 615 Mill Street, Half Moon Bay. 726-8750; (800) 900-ROSE. Fax: 726-3031. Website: www.millroseinn.com. $$$-$$$$

Zaballa House

When Estanislao Zaballa built his house in the 1850's on Main Street, it must have been considered quite a mansion by the locals. The structure, the oldest in Half Moon Bay, now contains a five bedroom bed and breakfast. Surrounding the original house is Zaballa Square, a well-integrated, patio-rich shopping center; eighteen additional inn rooms and suites are on a second floor. The rooms in the older house feature high-ceilings, wainscotting, clawfoot bath tubs, antique beds, pretty print wallpaper, and fluffy comforters which give the rooms an elegant "old fashioned" look. All rooms have the modern niceties of queen-sized beds and private baths. Some of the newer accommodations also feature fireplaces and Jacuzzi tubs. Tempting breakfasts may include waffles, home-made muffins, fresh fruit and house-made granola; evening beverages and hors d'oeuvres are served in the attractive living room and dining room. Well-behaved pets are welcome; some wheelchair accessible rooms. The location is excellent, just steps away from shops and restaurants. 324 Main Street, Half Moon Bay. 726-9123. Website: www.whistler.com/zaballa. $-$$$$

San Benito House

Days of "Gun Smoke" are relived in the old-west motif of the San Benito House Bed and Breakfast. Climb a steep staircase leading off the 1905 saloon to twelve rooms authentically, yet comfortably, decorated to carry out the theme. Fresh flowers from the surrounding gardens and pleasant aromas from the popular restaurant and deli below add to the ambiance. Some rooms share a bath; price includes a continental breakfast and a 10% discount at the San Benito House Restaurant. A large deck and pretty gazebo area are often used for weddings. Central downtown location at 356 Main Street, Half Moon Bay. 726-3425. $-$$

Old Thyme Inn

If you have ever enjoyed an authentic English bed and breakfast, you'll appreciate the Old Thyme Inn. An herb garden surrounds this charmingly restored Queen Anne Victorian. Choose from the Oregano Room, the Lavender Room, the Garden Suite, or any one of the seven bedrooms, all done meticulously in the herb motif. Fresh flowers in the rooms add to a pleasant bonhommie. Several rooms have fireplaces, whirlpool tubs, hyper allergic featherbeds. A full breakfast is served in a cheerful dining room. The fragrant back garden is frequently used for small weddings and special events. 779 Main Street, Half Moon Bay. 726-1616 or (800) 720-4277. Fax: 726-6394. E-mail: oldthyme@coastside.net. Website: www.oldthymeinn.com. $-$$$$

Old Thyme Inn

Cameron's Restaurant & Inn B & B

In this case the B & B refers to Bed & Beverage, appropriately so, since this inn is above a popular English pub-style restaurant. The three rooms all have queen beds and are reminiscent of an English road-side inn; two of the rooms share a bath. A double-decker London bus (serves as a smoking room) and a Chinese junk boat in the parking lot, assorted British post boxes and phone booths, and volley ball courts outback add to the fun. 1410 South Highway 1, Half Moon Bay. 726-5705. Fax: 726-9613. $

Plum Tree Court

Staying longer? How about your own private cottage set next to a charming courtyard and private patio? Decorative tile, wood burning stoves, and overstuffed leather living room furniture make this a very comfortable hide-away. Add to this all the modern amenities, including a well-stocked kitchen and your own laundry room, dishwasher, TV and VCR. Six one-bedroom cottages available by the week or by the month. Located downtown at 642 Johnston Street, Half Moon Bay. 712-0104. $-$$$

Half Moon Bay Lodge

The Half Moon Bay Lodge is a pleasant contemporary California mission style building located on Highway 1, overlooking a championship golf course with distant ocean views. Most of the eighty rooms have fireplaces and views, and all are impeccably clean and cheerful. Continental breakfast is included. This is a full service meeting facility and also features concierge service, glass enclosed whirlpool spas, heated swimming pool, and fitness center. Wheelchair accessible. 2400 South Highway 1, Half Moon Bay. 726-9000; (800)368-2468; Fax: 726-7951; e-mail: hmb@woodsidehotels.com. Website: www.woodsidehotels.com. $-$$$

Holiday Inn Express

The green-tiled roof Holiday Inn Express has a convenient Highway 1 location south of Highway 92 intersection and within walking distance of several restaurants. The fifty-two rooms are comfortably decorated and include continental breakfast; some rooms are wheelchair accessible. 230 Highway 1, Half Moon Bay. 726-3400; Fax: 726-1256. $-$$

Ramada Limited

Ramada Limited is a twenty-seven unit Spanish motif roadside motel. Clean and comfortable, it is near beaches but two miles to town. Continental breakfast included. Wheelchair accessible rooms available; no views. 3020 Highway 1, Half Moon Bay, near Miramar. 726-9700 or (800) 350-9888; Fax: 726-5269. Website: www.ramada.com.$-$$$

MID-COAST:

Beach House Inn & Conference Center

Unless you are bunking on a ship, you can't sleep any closer to the surf than at the Beach House Inn. Built right on the bluffs overlooking Pillar Point Harbor, the Inn is a very upscale "beach house". The fifty-four suites all include wood-burning fireplaces, wetbars, microwave ovens, two phone lines with fax, modem and voicemail, and all the other luxuries associated with world-class accommodations. A swimming pool, hot tub and pretty patio are screened off from nearby Highway 1. All suites have private patios or balconies, most have ocean views; continental breakfast is included. Four completely equipped meeting rooms are available. Wheelchair accessible rooms available. 4100 North Highway 1, Half Moon Bay, near Miramar. 712-0220; (800) 315-9366; Fax: 712-0693. Website: www.beach-house.com. $$$-$$$$

Seal Cove Inn

Take an elegant manor house that appears to have been plucked from the European countryside and place it within view of the ocean and a grove of wind-buffeted cypress trees. This is the Seal Cove Inn, a lavish country inn, beautifully appointed and situated near the Fitzgerald Marine Reserve in Moss Beach. Antique furniture mixed with stylish fabrics richly set off the vaulted ceilings and French doors that open onto the partial ocean views. All ten of the impeccably decorated rooms have private fireplaces and baths; the two suites have whirlpool tubs. A meeting room that includes audio visual equipment is available for up to fifteen participants. This is a versatile inn with atmosphere appropriate for either an executive retreat or the romantic couple. 221 Cypress Avenue, Moss Beach. 728-4114. Fax: 728-4116. E-mail: sealcove@coastside.net. Website: www.sealcoveinn.com. $$$-$$$$

Cypress Inn

Life at the Cypress Inn is a beach experience, albeit an elegant one. This is a bed and breakfast where almost all rooms include fireplaces, Jacuzzi tubs, and private decks with ocean views. The Inn is located on a bluff over looking the ocean, with easy walking to a wide stretch of beach. The twelve rooms are colorful and comfortably decorated with native folk art and a Southwest motif. A gourmet breakfast and afternoon wine, tea, and hors d'oeuvres are included in the price. Wheelchair accessible rooms available. 407 Mirada Road, Half Moon Bay, on Miramar Beach. 726-6002; (800) 832-3224; Fax: 712-0380. E-mail: lodging@cypressinn.com. Website: www.cypressinn.com. $$$-$$$$

Pillar Point Inn

Princeton-by-the-Sea. The name summons up visions of Cape Cod fishing villages, rambling gray-and-white buildings, boat masts, fog horns, and pelicans diving in the surf. And this is what you will find at Pillar Point Harbor in Princeton. The Pillar Point Inn, adjacent to the Harbor, is a two-storied, blue gray building with white trim and is everyone's image of a coastal inn. Each of the eleven rooms has a fireplace, private bathroom (some have steam baths), a European-style feather bed, and a bay window overlooking the harbor and ocean. Complimentary breakfasts and afternoon beverages; wheelchair accessible rooms available. 380 Capistrano Drive, Princeton-by-the-Sea. 728-7377. (800) 400-8281; Fax: 728-8345. $$-$$$

Old Jail
Half Moon Bay

Pacific Victorian Bed and Breakfast

The Victorians actually never had such a comfortable place to stay, however, the Pacific Victorian Bed and Breakfast re-creates the furnishings and style of that era. Located about a block from the ocean, most of the second floor rooms have balconies and views. Full breakfasts are served in the formal dining room and evening wine and hors d'oeuvres are presented in the parlor. Four rooms with private baths. 325 Alameda Avenue, Miramar. 712-3900. Fax: 712-3905. $$$

Harbor House

Pillar Point Harbor is an actual working harbor and has a character all its own. Hidden among the boatyards and storage units lies the Harbor House, located on the water's edge. Most of the six private patios and decks are but a mere fishing pole away from the shoreline. The outstanding views, comfortable pine and wicker furniture, fluffy bed covers, and fireplaces in each room add up to a great get-away spot. Wheelchair accessible rooms available. A penthouse suite and full conference facilities are located in a building next door. 346 Princeton Avenue, Half Moon Bay, at Pillar Point Harbor. 728-1572; Fax: 728-8271. Website: www.harborhousebandb.com. $$-$$$

Goose and Turrets

The Goose and Turrets Bed and Breakfast is tucked away in Montara a few blocks inland from Highway 1. The exterior of the building, once the Spanish American War Veterans' Country Club, is a bit cool and crumbly. But inside is a warm and spacious book and art filled living room. The gracious proprietors out-do themselves with a different and delicious breakfast every morning. Original art and German federbetts adorn each of the five bedrooms, all with private baths. Full breakfast and afternoon tea are included. Airport or harbor pickup is available. 835 George Street, Montara. 728-5451. Fax: 728-0141. Rgmgt@montara.com. Website: www.montara.com/goose. $-$$

Harborview Inn

This attractive coastal gray and white motel has seventeen units and is within walking distance of Pillar Point Harbor. Each room is cheerfully decorated and has a bay window overlooking the harbor and ocean. Continental breakfast included. 11 Avenue Alhambra, El Granada. 726-2329. $-$$.

Landis Shores

Ocean-front Landis Shores is located on the bluffs overlooking Miramar Beach, one of the coastside's most desirable locations. The eight suites are wine-themed, each equipped with Jacuzzi, tiled private ocean-view deck, fireplace, TV, and VCR; a full gourmet breakfast, appetizers, and evening wine are included. A small exercise room and meeting room are also available. 211 Mirada Road, Miramar. Call directory assistance for telephone number. $$$$

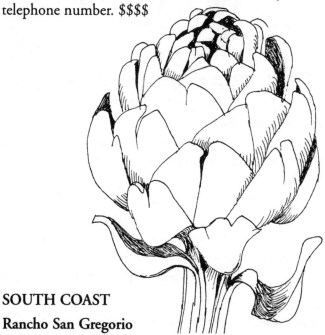

SOUTH COAST

Rancho San Gregorio

Past the artichoke fields and before the redwood parks, sits Rancho San Gregorio, a fifteen-acre ranch and country bed and breakfast inn. The Spanish style rancho overlooks pastures, apple orchards, and gardens, often used for company picnics and weddings. The public rooms and four bedrooms, all with private baths, present a comfortable image. Accommodations for children by prior arrangement. Breakfast included. 5086 La Honda Road, San Gregorio. 747-0810. Fax: 747-0184. E-mail: rsgleebud@aol.com. $

Pescadero Creekside Barn

In the 1870's, Pescadero was host to a multitude of visitors booked into two excellent hotels: the Swanton House and the Pescadero Hotel. Now downtown Pescadero has one cozy loft room for two people at the Pescadero Creekside Barn. It is located in a turn-of-the-century barn, and features a claw-foot tub, brass bed and gas fireplace. A real trip down memory lane. Two night minimum on weekends. 248 Stage Road, Pescadero. 879-0868. E-mail: 103406,2326@compuserve.com. $

Estancia del Mar

On a hillside, overlooking Pigeon Point Lighthouse, the Pacific Ocean, and miles of rich farmland, sits Estancia del Mar, a six unit hideaway situated on 4 ½ acres, about 30 miles south of Half Moon Bay. This is a good bet for wedding parties and other romantic weekends. Each one bedroom cottage features queen-sized beds, private baths, fully equipped kitchens and magnificent views. No telephones or TV's. Nightly, weekly, or monthly rentals. 460 Pigeon Point Road, Pescadero 879-1500: Fax: 583-8470. E-mail: ESTANCIADM@aol.com. $-$$$

The Lodge at Skylonda

A vigorous hike under majestic redwood trees starts the day at the ultimate spa and fitness center, The Lodge at Skylonda. This may be followed by a Swedish massage, aquatic exercises in the indoor pool, or perhaps tai-chi or yoga instructions. Enjoy healthy gourmet meals and appetizers served next to the massive stone fireplace in the redwood-paneled great room. Then retire to one of sixteen rustic, yet elegant, guestrooms featuring a deck or patio, soaking tubs and, of course, terry robes. This is the ultimate escape, meaning no TV's and telephones only by request. Located deep in the redwood forests at 16350 Skyline Blvd., Woodside. 851-6625. (800) 851-2222. Fax: 851-5504. $$$$

Costanoa at Cascade Ranch

Costanoa at Cascade Ranch is a combination rustic campground and posh resort, set on 480 acres next to the proposed Cascade Ranch State Park. This is upscale camping at its best and features a lodge with forty guest rooms and twelve private cabins all with private fireplaces and room service, eighty-eight deluxe tent cabins (equipped with down comforters), and forty-seven standard tent cabins. Additionally, there are spots for campers to pitch their own tents and for RV's, conference facilities, complete spa services, bike rentals, and a gourmet deli. (800) 738-7477.

B & B at Año Nuevo

Tucked in the pine trees, on the hillside overlooking Año Nuevo State Reserve, is a modified log home offering one cozy guest room. A separate entrance ensures privacy and the stone fireplace, country furniture, and magnificent views ensure comfort. A continental breakfast is included. The secluded property offers miles of hiking trails and picnic possibilities. Located across from Año Nuevo State Reserve off Highway 1. 879-1252. E-mail: 104434.2262@compuserve.com. $$$

Davenport Bed and Breakfast Inn

Davenport is actually not in San Mateo County, but it's proximity to Año Nuevo and its attractive features and coast setting warrant its inclusion. If you have ever longed to hide out in complete obscurity, this is the place. Thirty-six miles south of Half Moon Bay and twelve miles north of Santa Cruz, Davenport is a small, occasionally dusty but charming mining company town with a popular restaurant, intriguing shops, and the Davenport Bed and Breakfast Inn. Four of the rooms are housed in a small building next to the restaurant and eight rooms are above the Cash Store and Restaurant. All the artistically furnished rooms have private baths. Breakfast is included in the moderate rates. 31 Davenport Avenue, Davenport. (408) 425-1818, (800) 870-1817; Fax: (408) 423-1160. E-mail: Inn@swanton.com. Website: www.swanton.com. $-$$

PACIFICA

Best Western Lighthouse

Close enough to the surf to hear the waves at night, this hotel has a wonderful location. The Best Western Lighthouse is an attractive, multistoried, modern, weathered-woodsided hotel with over ninety guest rooms and suites and excellent meeting facilities. Many of the rooms have stunning ocean views; some have fireplaces. The meeting rooms are frequently used for company meetings, weddings, and other special occasions. The facilities also include a pool, Jacuzzi, sauna, and gym. 105 Rockaway Beach Avenue, Pacifica. 355-6300; (800) 832-4777; Fax: 355-9217. E-mail: lhthse@aol.com. $$-$$$

Days Inn

Across the street from the Best Western Lighthouse, and one half block from the beach, this motor inn with a Victorian facade is clean and comfortable. There are forty-one rooms, several have ocean views. Adjacent to several restaurants. 200 Rockaway Beach Avenue, Pacifica. 359-7700. $-$$

Montara Lighthouse Hostel

HOSTELS

MID-COAST

Montara Lighthouse Hostel

The Montara Lighthouse, sitting on the cliff overlooking the ocean, has a location hotel managers dream about. The hostel can accommodate forty-nine people and features a hot tub, bike rentals, two kitchens, and beach access. The maximum stay is three nights. You are expected to pitch in and do chores in the morning before you depart. Gates are open from 7:30 a.m. to 9:30 a.m. and 4:30 p.m. to 9:30 p.m. daily. Prices are very inexpensive. Highway 1 at 16th Street, Montara. 728-7177. Website: www.norcalhostels.org. SEE: Seeing chapter for additional information on the Lighthouse.

SOUTH COAST

Pigeon Point Lighthouse Hostel

This frequently photographed 115-foot lighthouse is beautifully positioned on the coastal edge. The forty bed hostel has a kitchen for the culinary inclined. Nearby on the beach are tidepools and good surf fishing. Maximum stay is three nights. Inexpensive prices make this is a very popular stop. Reservations are recommended at least one week in advance. Call 879-0633 during desk hours which are 7:30 a.m. to 9:30 a.m.; 4:30 p.m. to 9:30 p.m. daily. Located seven miles south of Pescadero, off Highway 1, on Pigeon Point Road. Website: www.norcalhostels.org. SEE: The Seeing chapter for additional information on the Lighthouse.

RV PARKS

HALF MOON BAY

Pelican Point RV Park

The secluded country setting of this fully equipped RV park gives it a look of permanence. It is nicely landscaped and adjacent to a championship 18 hole golf course and cliffs overlooking the ocean. Facilities include seventy-five full hook-up sites, cable TV, laundry room, LP gas, picnic tables, store, and disposal station. Tent camping is also permitted. 1001 Miramontes Point Road, Half Moon Bay. 726-9100.

RV, Pelican Point RV Park

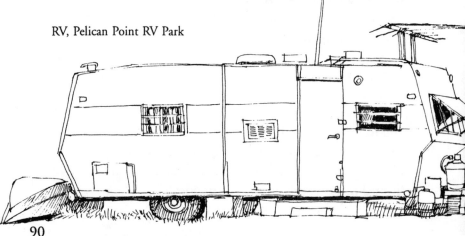

MID-COAST

Pillar Point RV Park

This newly refurbished RV park, wedged between Highway 1 and Pillar Point Harbor, offers plenty of picnic tables and barbecue pits, upgraded wheelchair accessible restrooms, and landscaping. Campers look over a sandy beach. No reservations; fees are paid at the lot. Located at the breakwater, adjacent to Surfers' Beach at 4000 Highway 1, in El Granada.

PACIFICA

Pacific Park RV Resort

The Pacific Park RV Resort is located on the cliffs overlooking the ocean although the "overlooking" is for only the first row of RV's. The fully equipped, modern RV park offers hookups for 216 RV's, heated swimming pool, arcade, LP gas, and RV supplies on the premises. There is easy access to bus service and BART, and it is near restaurants and car rentals. 700 Palmetto Avenue, Pacifica. 355-7093; In State: (800) 992-0554. Out of State: (800) 822-1250; Fax: 355-7102. Website: www.miramarhotels.com/pacificpark.

CAMPING

HALF MOON BAY

Francis Beach

Francis Beach is one of the few beaches in the area where you can camp on the sand. By day the campground offers excellent family beaching activities and good surfing. This is a state beach campground with fifty-one tent and RV campsites, wheelchair-accessible restrooms, weekly campfire programs, and picnic tables. No RV hookups are available; cold outdoor showers. Parking fee. Dogs on a leash are allowed. No reservations, first come-first served; for information call 726-8820; (800) 444-7275. West on Highway 1 at Kelly Avenue in Half Moon Bay. Website: www.park-net.com.

Sweetwood Group Camp

For group camping on the beach, try Sweetwood State Beach. It is exclusively for group rentals and can accommodate up to fifty people for tent camping or day use. The gated beach area offers stretches of sandy beach, buffeted from Highway 1 by a grove of trees. On Highway 1 north of Half Moon Bay, across from Frenchmen's Creek housing development. Reservations: (800) 444-7275.

SOUTH COAST

San Mateo Memorial County Park

For the ethereal experience of camping under the redwoods, San Mateo Memorial County Park is a sure bet. This county campground has over 100 campsites for families; it also offers picnic facilities, a visitors center, camp store, a creek swimming area, campfire programs, group areas and trails. First come-first served for families; reservations required for all youth groups. Eleven miles east of Pescadero on Pescadero Road. For information call 879-0210. SEE: Adventuring chapter for more information on the Park.

Portolá State Park

Another popular redwood forested state park, Portolá, offers fifty-two campsites and three hike-in group-camping areas. There are many miles of hiking trails in this beautiful park. The park has hot showers but no RV hookups. Weekend reservations recommended. Go east on Highway 84 (La Honda Road). Take Pescadero Road to Alpine Road. Turn on to Portolá State Park Road. 948-9098; (800) 444-7275. Website: www.park-net.com. SEE: Adventuring chapter for additional information on the Park.

Butano State Park

Redwoods, shady glens of ferns, and wildlife add to the backwoods experience of this impressive 2200 acre state park. Butano has forty campsites with tables and stoves. It offers miles of hiking trails, some with scenic views of Año Nuevo Island, fishing, hiking, picnicking, guided nature walks, and weekend campfire programs during the summer. Butano has no showers and no hook ups for RV's, however, RV camping is permitted with limits of 24 feet for travel trailers and 27 feet for motor homes. For reservations call 879-2040; (800) 444-7275. Seven miles south of Pescadero on Cloverdale Road. SEE: Adventuring chapter for additional information on the Park.

Sam McDonald Park

Sam McDonald is a redwood forested county park that offers camping for youth groups and campers with horses only. A hikers' hut, for up to fourteen people, is run by the Sierra Club and can be rented by the night. Located about 1 3/4 miles from Sam McDonald Park parking lot. For reservations call 494-9901. SEE: Adventuring for additional information on the Park.

7

EATING

For Northern Californians, eating out has become a first order event. More knowledgeable diners, a greater variety of various national cuisines, more attention to the proper roots of American cooking, a focus on fresh ingredients and fresh flavors, and just plain better cooking are in.

Coastside dining mirrors these trends. Eating out in coastal spots has become more an event for anticipating good food and less a step into culinary darkness. You will now find good California food in old inn settings, a wave of more stylized Italian cooking served in sleek surroundings, and improved seafood preparations presented in a variety of atmospheric spots ranging from coastal inn to cliff hanging modern. Enjoy the Coastside's culinary renaissance.

For each restaurant we describe the type of food, the setting, the house specialties, and the price range. We list only those spots we have tried and liked. Prices, and for that matter quality, can change quickly; a new chef, a new owner, or an increase in ingredient costs can turn today's gourmet bargain into tomorrow's overpriced dining disaster. Noting this caveat, we use the dollar sign symbols ($$) to represent price category. Prices are for a per-person meal, not including beverage, service, or tax.

$	Inexpensive	Under $10
$$	Moderate	$10 to $20
$$$	Moderately Expensive	$20 to $30
$$$$	Expensive	$30 and up

Restaurants are listed alphabetically, by area. They are followed by a listing of coffee houses, snack bars, and delicatessens. We start with the restaurants of Half Moon Bay and then move to the Mid-Coast, the South Coast, and Pacifica.

RESTAURANTS
HALF MOON BAY

Bangkok House
Sample well prepared and artistically presented Thai food in a comfortable, tastefully decorated dining room. Leaded glass windows, spaciously placed tables, and a fireplace contribute to your sense of comfort. Bangkok House is a very good stop for curries, satays, prawn and vegetable soup, and a wide variety of other Thai dishes both mild and fiery. Open Tuesday through Sunday for lunch and dinner. 225 South Highway 1 in Shoreline Station. 726-5247. $$

Cameron's Restaurant and Inn

Hey matie! This "British pub" bills itself as "your local family neighborhood pub & grub" and that is a very good description. Grab one of 18 beers on tap, or a shake from the full soda fountain, a basket of fish and chips or a burger and fries, and enter a dart game. Local entertainment some nights. A double decker bus in the parking lot serves as a unique smoking area. Open daily for lunch and dinner. 1410 South Highway 1. 726-5705. $

Chateau des Fleurs

French cuisine is served in this cozy Victorian house. Specialties include classical French dishes like rabbit sautéed in red wine and duck pate with Grand Marnier, but the menu features chicken, steaks, veal, lamb and seafood prepared in lighter sauces. Here's a French restaurant you can come to in your casual coastside clothes and better yet, pay only casual money for a good meal. Open daily for lunch and dinner. 523 Church Street. 712-8837. $$

El Perico

The landmark spreading cypress tree is gone, but El Perico remains conveniently located at the entrance to Half Moon Bay on Highway 92. The restaurant has an attractive woody interior and serves Mexican food with standard south of the border dinner specials. Open daily for lunch and dinner. Popular bar. 211 Highway 92. 726-3737. $

It's Italia Pizzeria

Not only does this sleek Italian eatery serve the best pizza in town, they also serve very good pastas and salads. Pizzas might include artichoke hearts, caramelized onions, shitake mushrooms, Italian sausage, Mozzarella, and many other choices; the Pasta Primavera is another favorite, cooked to perfection and sprinkled with asiago cheese. Open daily for lunch and dinner. Located at 40 Stone Pine Center, off Main Street. 726-4444. $

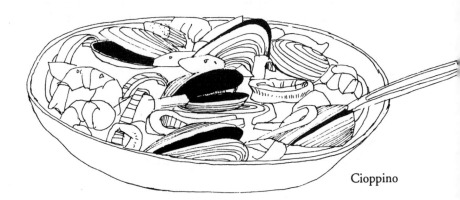

Cioppino

Pasta Moon

How do skewers of homemade Italian sausage with rosemary and chicken breast, fettucine with smoked salmon, and linguine with prawns in a saffron cream sauce sound? Pasta Moon serves these and many other fashionable Italian dishes. You will like the food, the California-Italian clubby atmosphere, and the smooth service. Views of downtown Half Moon Bay can be seen from the trattoria style tables. Pasta Moon is a stylish and comfortable spot and open daily for lunch and dinner. Tin Palace, 315 Main Street. 726-5125. $$$

San Benito House
California touched food served in a charming and comfortable old country inn mark the San Benito House. The very good homemade breads and multi-ingredient salads are particularly good openers to the changing entrees. The Garden Deli, facing Main Street, specializes in large tasty sandwiches. A pretty garden and expansive deck serve both restaurant and deli. The restaurant is open Thursday to Saturday for dinner and for Sunday brunch; The deli is open daily for lunch. 356 Main Street. 726-3425. $-$$$

Siam Restaurant
Satays, jumbo prawns stuffed with ground shrimp, Thai peanut salad, and chicken coconut milk soup, all quite good, are served in this attractive roadside restaurant. The owners provide a warm and inviting welcome, the family style ambience and charming Thai decor are very pleasant, but it is the food that will draw you back for return visits. Open daily for lunch and dinner. 108 North Highway 1. 712-0583. $

Souper Dooper
Soup aficionados take heed. Several varieties of steaming bowls of homemade soups, including excellent clam chowder and minestrone, are prepared at Souper Dooper. Tasty burgers, sandwiches, salads, including homestyle potato salad, round out the menu. The interior has a Southwestern warmth, and features original art work on the walls, a cozy fireplace, and a very friendly staff. Open daily from 11:30 a.m. to 6 p.m. 328 Main Street in Zaballa Square. 560-4880. $

Spanishtown Mexican Restaurant

Located in a small older house which includes an enclosed glassed front patio area, Spanishtown is appropriately atmospheric with serapes, sombreros, and bull fighting posters hung throughout. Good combination plates will satisfy most diners, but also try the more unusual fish, rabbit, and goat preparations. The service is attentive and the portions large. Fruity sangrias and Mexican soft drinks sooth the fire. Open daily for lunch and dinner. 515 Church Street. 726-7357. $

Sushi Main Street

Sushi Main Street is one of the most attractive (and busiest) restaurants in Half Moon Bay. Japanese food is the focus, but artifacts and decor from Indonesia give the restaurant a kind of Asian inn ambiance. The house specialty is sushi of all kinds; a full range of other equally tasty Japanese items are also served. Open daily for lunch and dinner. 696 Mill Street. 726-6336. $-$$

Three Amigos

Simple excellent Mexican food and tunes from South of the border await the visitor to this cantina on the coast. The giant "wet" burritos are a hit, but the fajita and chili relleno combinations are also good choices in this popular gathering place. Open daily from 10 a.m. to 10 p.m. 200 South Highway 1. 726-6080. $

Two Fools Cafe and Market

Looking for American food, like meat loaf with garlic mashed potatoes, or a top notch vegetarian meal? Two Fools is calling you. The well executed California cuisine is served in a popular and comfortable downtown location. Open daily for lunch and dinner except closed Mondays for dinner. 408 Main Street. 712-1222. $

MID-COAST

Anchorage

The Anchorage is well situated on the edge of Pillar Point Harbor, and most of the tables enjoy expansive ocean and coastal mountain views. This, together with the mouth watering good fish preparations (from sand dabs to sushi to bouillabaisse), make the Anchorage a standout. The elegant chowder house atmosphere, popular bar, and outdoor patio area are bonuses. Open daily for lunch and dinner; Sunday brunch. 4210 North Highway 1, El Granada. 726-2822. $$-$$$

Barbara's Fish Trap

Barbara's Fish Trap is one of the coast's most popular fish restaurants. The pier setting and coastal bric-a-brac along with the outstanding views sets the right mood for waterside dining. The restaurant serves a large variety of fresh fish, mostly grilled or fried, and enjoys a funky elbows-on-the-table atmosphere. Outdoor seating is also available. Open daily for lunch and dinner. No credit cards accepted. Capistrano Road, Princeton. 728-7049. $$

Cafe Classique

Cafe Classique is a brightly painted gourmet-to-go restaurant, with an ever-changing menu of unique breakfast and sandwich specialties and coffees. The food is quite tasty and the interior a rainbow of colors. Open from 5 a.m. to 3 p.m. daily. Located on Sevilla Avenue, northeast of the stoplight on Highway 1, in El Granada. 726-9775. $

Café Gibraltar

Fast becoming a Coastside favorite, this small restaurant serves imaginative and well prepared dishes all Mediterranean inspired. The mixed antipasti platter with housemade flatbread amply serves two; entrees such as clams sautéed with Spanish chorizo, or wild mushroom risotto are artistically presented. An outside sitting area adjoins the cafe. Open daily for dinner; closed Tuesdays. Corner of 7th and Highway l, Montara. 728-9030. $-$$.

Chart House

California contemporary cuisine and a striking Pacific-modern interior and wood shingled exterior architecture highlight the Chart House. It is situated on a bluff overlooking the ocean, rocky cliffs, and a pristine undeveloped beach. Well prepared in-vogue food is offered: fresh fish, grilled chicken and steaks, and a benchmark salad bar. Access to Montara State Beach for after dinner walks is a plus for the romantic. The Chart House has an ocean view lounge and oyster bar and is open daily for dinner. 8150 Highway 1, Montara. 728-7366. $$-$$$

Demi Lune

Demi Lune sports a wide menu of aptly titled "California Coastside Continental" cuisine. It enjoys a warm glow and comfortable ambiance at night, where red table cloths, pleasant settings, and attentive service compliment the wide choice of interesting appetizers, pastas, meats and excellent seafood preparations such as pistachio encrusted halibut and moist battered sole. Very good overall value. Open for dinner Wednesday through Sunday and for weekend brunch. 3048 North Highway 1, in Miramar. 726-8114. $$-$$$

Highway One Diner

Highway One Diner carries off a 1950's motif from food to abundant and clever '50's memorabilia spread from ceiling to floor. Excellent harbor views are a bonus. Hamburgers, hot dogs, fried chicken with mashed potatoes and gravy, and other all American foods are served. Open daily for breakfast, lunch and dinner; closed Mondays. 4230 Highway 1, El Granada. 726-9500. $-$$.

Ketch Joanne and Harbor Bar

If you like coastside hangouts specializing in good fresh seafood and large breakfasts, you'll like Ketch Joanne's. The woody, ship like interior with hatch covers, racing shell with oars, and whale pictures sparks the interior. The potbelly stove and local fishermen add color. The fish dishes are well prepared, and the popular bar offers occasional live entertainment. Open daily for breakfast, lunch, and dinner. Pillar Point Harbor, Princeton. 728-3747. $-$$

Mezza Luna

Tuscany comes to Pillar Point Harbor and settles at the Old Princeton Inn, now reincarnated as Mezza Luna. The orange and gold stucco walls and spacious interior set the perfect mood for the authentic trattoria menu. Fresh bread, pizza and deserts are made on the premises and match well prepared pastas, sauces, roasted meats and fresh tangy salads. The calamari fritti (lightly battered calamari) is the best on the coast. A full cocktail bar and large dance floor and lounge are popular on weekends when live entertainment is offered. Open daily for lunch and dinner. 459 Prospect Way, Princeton. 728-8108. $$-$$$

Miramar Beach Inn

Located practically right on the water, the Miramar was once a Prohibition roadhouse. Now, large picture windows overlook the spectacular ocean scenery from a pleasant wood paneled interior dining room and lounge. The innovative menu makes good use of local ingredients offering several seafood and steak specialties and dishes featuring artichokes. Open daily for lunch and dinner and Sundays for brunch. 131 Mirada Road, Miramar. 726-9053. $$-$$$

Cliff view,
Moss Beach

Moss Beach Distillery
The Distillery enjoys a cliff hugging Pacific setting, a speak-easy past, and a long rumored blue lady ghost. An expansive bar adjoins the restaurant. Entrees are rather expensive, focusing on fish, meat, and pasta. Consider the downstairs bar and light food area with deck chairs and blankets to share. A good date hangout. Open daily for lunch and dinner. Beach Way and Ocean Blvd, Moss Beach. 728-5595. $$-$$$

Princeton Seafood Company Market and Restaurant
Princeton is a friendly and nautically atmospheric place with perky service and tasty seafood. The clam chowder is a local Clam Chowder Cook-off winner and the many fish entrees are among the best prepared on the Coast. Princeton Seafood is frequently filled with local fishermen and residents; the ocean collectibles on the walls lend a pleasing harbor atmosphere. Open daily for lunch and dinner. Pillar Point Harbor, Princeton. 726-2722. $-$$

SOUTH COAST

Alice's Restaurant

Located on Skyline Blvd where Woodside Road and La Honda Road intersect, Alice's has been a stop for motorcyclists, hikers, and lovers of the great outdoors for years. Alice's is in a wooden cabin with a spacious deck for outside seating and good views of the towering redwoods. Sandwiches and breakfasts are simple but ample, good, and reasonably priced. Open for breakfast and lunch daily. 851-0303. $

Duarte's

Step into the old west atmosphere of Duarte's, featuring wooden floors and local cowboys hanging out at the great old bar. The food specialties are crab cioppino, abalone, and artichoke dishes. Homemade pies and chili verdi and artichoke soups are delicious and can be eaten there or are available to go. Weekends are exceptionally busy as this is a destination restaurant for Bay Area residents. Open daily for breakfast, lunch, and dinner. 202 Stage Road, Pescadero. 879-0464. $$

The New Davenport Cash Store and Restaurant

Delicious waffles, muffins, and other homemade baked goods tempt you as you walk into this homey wood floored restaurant and craft shop. The restaurant is located thirty-six miles south of Half Moon Bay and is open daily for breakfast, lunch, and dinner. 31 Davenport Avenue. (408) 425-1818. $

PACIFICA

Invitation House

You know you are in for a treat the moment you enter the Invitation House. The chic decor, spacious setting, attentive staff, and large Korean clientele are the tip off. The Korean and Japanese menu is exhaustive, so let your waiter be your guide. The food is quite good with various Korean combination barbecue specials. Open daily for lunch and dinner. 270 Rockaway Beach Avenue. 738-8588. $-$$

Wine and Calamari

Moonraker Restaurant

The Moonraker is the premier view restaurant in Pacifica and is one of the Coastside's most romantic dining spots. All of the seating faces the picture windows overlooking the Pacific. At night, spots light the crashing waves below. Soft music and lighting are atmospheric. The food has been both very good, and very ordinary, depending on current ownership; lately, it has been good. The view alone is worth a try. Open for dinner daily. 105 Rockaway Beach. 359-0303. $$$

Mr. Lee's Chinese Food

The lighthouse shaped building at the entrance to Pedro Point stands as a beacon to some very good Chinese cooking and a very pleasant interior. Mr. Lee, formerly of the Pedro Point Restaurant, offers a wide array of freshly prepared entrees, particularly fish dishes as well as a daily dim sum menu (for lunch only), and a cheery greeting and commentary. Good food and fun talk are the specialties here. Open daily for lunch and dinner; food to go available. 5560 Highway 1. 359-9085. $-$$

Nick's Seashore Restaurant

Wave level views and California coastal dining circa the 1950's mark Nick's. Settle into the tufted banquettes and try the scalone or other specialties. There is an active lounge area and large banquet space for group meals. Nick's is open daily for breakfast, lunch, and dinner and frequently has nightly entertainment. 100 Rockaway Beach. 359-3900. $$

Ristorante Mare

Pedro Point is vaguely reminiscent of Italy's Portifino and now they have a very good trattoria. The Ristorante Mare serves authentic Northern Italian cuisine, including a mouth watering minestrone, roasted meats, and a variety of pastas in an atmospheric inn-like setting. Open daily for lunch and dinner; closed Mondays. 404 San Pedro Avenue. 355-5980. $-$$

Rock'n Robs

When was the last time you had a real milkshake served in a frosty silver goblet? Rock'n Robs is an old fashion diner serving ample hamburgers and milkshakes among '50's memorabilia. Open daily for lunch and dinner. Located at Rockaway Beach, 450 Dondee Way. 359-FOOD. $

Tams Cuisine of China

Tam's sharp interior is a well appointed back drop for the Chinese cooking. Pink table linens, nice flower arrangements and artwork, and brisk efficient service add to the upscale atmosphere. Slightly spicy orange-flavored prawns are good, as are many of the vegetable dishes. Open daily for lunch and dinner. 494 Manor Plaza. 359-7575. $$

DELIS, SNACKBARS AND COFFEE HOUSES
HALF MOON BAY

Cunha Country Store

This country store with wooden floors and delicious deli smells provides luncheon meat sandwiches, fresh local produce, and a selection of groceries. No seating. Open daily from 8 a.m. to 8 p.m. Main Street and Kelly Avenue. 726-4071.

Half Moon Bay Coffee Company

Half Moon Bay Coffee is a busy coffee house cum breakfast and lunch bar, with lots of locals, a real buzz of activity, and an excellent selection of snacks. Indoor and outdoor seating available. Open daily from 6 a.m. to 9 p.m. Located on the corner of Main Street and Stone Pine Road. 726-3664.

Healing Moon

The Healing Moon specializes in wholesome fresh and organic deli lunches, hot soups, and fresh sandwiches. Eat in the charming enclosed back garden. Open daily from 10 a.m. to 6 p.m. 523 Main Street. 726-7881.

LA-DI-DA

LA-DI-DA is a stylish coffee house which makes good use of its long, narrow space. The cleverly designed and painted furniture and artwork on the walls make this an appealing place to gather for coffee, desserts, and lunches. Weekend entertainment. Open daily until 7 p.m. on weekdays and 6 p.m. on weekends. 500C Purissima. 726-0306.

M. Coffee's

You will find M. Coffee's a leading place in town for a cup of steaming fresh brewed coffee, cappuccino, or espresso. Very good coffee beans and light snacks are also available. Picnic supplies such as cheese, pates, and crackers are on hand. The barn-like but comfortable interior is usually full of interesting looking people. Open daily from 7 a.m. to 6 p.m.; weekends 9 a.m. to 6 p.m. 522 Main Street. 726-6241.

Moonside Bakery and Cafe

Excellent pastries and breads, pizza cooked in a wood-burning oven, sandwiches and salads, along with expresso and other coffee drinks are served in La Piazza covered mall or out on the sidewalk. Open daily from 7 a.m. to 6 p.m.; closed Tuesdays. 604 Main Street. 726-9070.

The Rotisserie Market

The large rotisserie oven, slowly roasting pork, chicken, lamb and beef, is the centerpiece of this small take-out eatery. Besides the mouth watering meats, also try the salads and other tempting side dishes. Open daily for lunch and dinner. 315 Main Street. 712-7400.

MID-COAST

Creekside Smoke House

Smoked albacore, salmon, trout, sturgeon and other fish are prepared and sold at the tiny Creekside Smoke House. Wonderful salmon jerky and various seafood salads also sold. Open daily except Mondays from 10 a.m. to 6 p.m. Closed September, January and February. 280 Avenue Alhambra, El Granada. 712-8862.

El Granada Hardware Store

This is hardly a typical coffee house, but El Granada Hardware has very good coffee and sandwiches and light snacks. While you drink your coffee you can use their xerox or send a fax, shop for hardware items, or learn much about the coast from the proprietor. Open daily. 85 Avenue Portola, El Granada. 726-5009.

SOUTH COAST

Kings Mountain Country Store

This is an atmospheric and well-equipped stop for picnic supplies while hiking on and around Skyline. Kings Mountain Store has a large wine selection, homemade salads and sandwiches as well as many gift items. Take a look at the informative history wall. 13100 Skyline Blvd, Woodside. 851-3852.

Norm's Market

A wonderful selection of hot out-of-the-oven breads, cheeses, wines, and other picnic and deli items greets the eye and nose. Artichoke bread is a local favorite. 287 Stage Road, Pescadero. 879-0147.

Skywood Trading Post and Deli

Picnic tables outside, deli sandwiches and other fresh foods inside and you have a great stop for lunch. Open daily. Skyline Blvd at Highway 84 in Woodside. 851-0914.

PACIFICA

Beach Cafe and Deli

Vegetarian items and salads are the specialty. The deli is conveniently located just north of Rockaway Beach at 4430 Coast Highway. Open daily from 9 a.m. to 5 p.m. 355-4532.

Mazzetti's Bakery

Mazzetti's is a family owned and operated landmark in Pacifica. The specialties are honey raisin bran muffins, Italian rum cake, pastries, and focaccia bread. Try one, along with a cup of steaming coffee, for a very satisfying break. Open daily from 5 a.m. to 6 p.m. 101 Manor Drive. 355-1007.

El Grano de Oro

El Grano de Oro brings a South of the border touch as they make and sell delicious fresh-from-the-oven tortillas, stacked and ready to go to market. Open daily; closed Sundays. 1710 Francisco Blvd. 355-8417.

8

ENTERTAINING

Entertainment on the Coastside is widespread, varied, and usually foot-stomping good. Annual events celebrate everything from pumpkins to chili to the fog. Because of the rural nature of the community these are down-home folksy events and many of them are free.

This Side of the Hill Players and Pacifica Spindrift Players (both theater groups) present first-rate performances. Concerts with nationally known jazz and classical artists appear at the Bach Dancing & Dynamite Society; stand up comedy, rock and roll, top forties hits, and country and western music is performed with style and vigor at several local establishments. But the top entertainer on the Coastside is the natural setting itself; it is the perfect back drop for special events such as weddings, corporate meetings and group picnics.

In this chapter are listed the annual events, performing arts, pubs and clubs, and the best gathering places.

ANNUAL EVENTS

ALL YEAR LONG

Flower Market

Rows and rows of white and lavender stock, fields of heather, and hillsides covered in white and yellow marguerites remind the visitor that this is one of America's premier flower growing areas. The local flower growers and wholesalers sell directly to the public once a month at the Flower Market.

Besides fresh cut flowers, you can buy potted plants, bedding plants, dried flowers, foliage, and a few craft items. Street music and entertainment add to the festive aura. The Flower Market is held the third Saturday of each month throughout the year from 10 a.m. to 4 p.m. From May through September, the market is held outdoors at Kelly Avenue and Main Street. The rest of the year, the market is held in La Piazza, 604 Main Street, Half Moon Bay.

SPRING

Chamarita

For many years Portuguese immigrants, mainly from the Azores, have made the Coastside their home. Chamarita, a traditional Azores-Portuguese festival, is one of the many treasurers the Portuguese population has introduced to this area.

Legend holds that centuries ago a mysterious ship appeared to provide food for the inhabitants of the famine-stricken Azores without asking for payment in return. Now people of Azore-Portuguese descent feed the towns people of their communities once each year and conduct a festival to celebrate their historic good fortune.

Colorful marching bands, Portuguese flags, silver-and-leather-clad equestrian groups, and queens with white lace ballgowns lead off the annual parade. In Half Moon Bay, they parade down Main Street to the Catholic Church and return one hour

later to the I.D.E.S. Hall. The Half Moon Bay Festival is held the seventh Sunday after Easter; call 726-5202 for more information. The festival is held in Pescadero the sixth Sunday after Easter. Call 726-5701 for additional information on the Pescadero Chamarita.

Spring Fest and Auction
Hundreds of items, from weekend travel packages to handmade doll houses, are up for auction to benefit the Pacifica Co-op Nursery School. The festival is held in March at the Pacifica Community Center. 355-4465.

Artichoke Golf Classic
This golf tournament sponsored by the Half Moon Bay Chamber of Commerce is held at the Half Moon Bay Golf Links in May. 726-8380.

Pacific Coast Dream Machine
Old cars, planes, engines, tractors, and all kinds of machines are on display along with food, games, and entertainment. This event is held at the Half Moon Bay Airport in April to benefit the Coastside Adult Day Health Care Center. An entrance fee is charged. 726-2328.

SUMMER

La Honda Country Fair and Music Festival
Go for good ol' knee-slapping music, local crafts, and lots of fun under the redwoods. La Honda Gardens is the location of this annual music and crafts fair. Generally held the second weekend of June. 747-0965.

Coastside Bluff Top Walk, Run, Roll
Sign up to walk, run, or ride a wheelchair along the Coastside Trail to help benefit the Senior Coastsiders. All ability levels are accommodated. Held in early Summer. 726-9056.

Fourth of July
The Coastside is a good place to spend the Fourth of July. An annual parade marches down Main Street, Half Moon Bay at 11 a.m. In the evening, community sponsored fireworks ignite over the breakwater at Pillar Point and are impressive as they light up the harbor area. 726-8380.

In Pacifica, the Fourth of July Fiesta is held at Frontierland Park at Yosemite Drive and Oddstad Blvd from 11 a.m. to 5 p.m. The event also includes food, concessions, entertainers, bands, and games. 738-7380.

Tours de Fleurs

Coastside nurseries open their doors to the public at this popular event sponsored by the Half Moon Bay Chamber of Commerce, in July. You can learn about the Coastside horticulture and tour the area at the same time. 726-8380.

Half Moon Bay Charity Golf Classic

This annual golf tournament draws sports celebrities and famous entertainers to benefit Seton Coastside Hospital. It is held at the Half Moon Bay Golf Links in July. 991-6448.

Pacifica Antique and Collectibles Street Fair

Over 100 dealers of antiques, collectibles, and memorabilia set up shop along Palmetto Avenue in Pacifica for a one-day event in July. This is a Lions' Club fund raiser. 355-4122.

Pescadero Arts and Fun Faire

Put on your cowboy hat and head for Pescadero the third weekend of August for the Pescadero Arts and Fun Faire. This music, food, and crafts festival benefits the South Coast Children's Services. 879-0848.

A Taste of Pacifica

Food, wine tasting, art, and music happen at Rockaway Beach in August. 355-4122.

FALL

King's Mountain Art Festival

For original art and very different kinds of craft items, come to this art festival at the King's Mountain Community Center on Skyline Blvd in Woodside. The art is displayed in a redwood grove, a perfect back drop. This well-organized event offers shuttle buses to the festival from parking spots along Skyline Blvd. It is usually held Labor Day weekend. 851-2710.

Harbor Day

This annual event is held at Pillar Point Harbor towards the end of September and is sponsored by the Half Moon Bay Fishermen's Marketing Association. A seafood barbecue, arts and crafts booths, entertainment and environmental education presentations are all part of the festivities. 728-0209.

Pacific Coast Fog Fest

All you have to do is hold a festival to honor the fog and the fog doesn't even show up. The sun usually shines at Fog Fest time in Pacifica; the town has never even won the "Foggiest City Contest." The festival begins with the popular "Discover Pacifica" parade on Saturday morning. During the two-day event there is a human fog calling contest, arts and crafts booths, food concessions (try a fog dog), classic car show, wine and beer gardens, and musical entertainers from Reggae to Rock. The Fog Fest is held in late September on Palmetto Avenue in Pacifica. 355-4122.

Half Moon Bay Art and Pumpkin Festival

On the third weekend of October the Great Pumpkin comes to Main Street, Half Moon Bay, along with 300,000 people from "over the hill" for the annual Arts and Pumpkin Festival. The arts and crafts are plentiful, but come for the wonderful food such as linguica, pickled Brussels sprouts, Welsh pasties, and all things pumpkin—ice cream, soup, bread, pies, and cookies. Other special events include the Great Pumpkin parade (held Saturday at noon), a ten kilometer pumpkin run, and a masquerade ball at the I.D.E.S. Hall on Saturday evening. Proceeds from the festival support several local charities. 726-9652.

Chili Cookoff

At Pillar Point Harbor, in October, town folk and restaurateurs try to outdo each other with the most unusual and delicious chilies. Tried alligator chili? This is a down-home event, featuring well known and local bands. Proceeds benefit the Coastside Opportunity Center. 726-9071.

WINTER

Stage Road Winter Faire

To celebrate the holidays in Pescadero, go the first weekend in December to Stage Road for arts and crafts, festive music, and lots of homemade baked goods. Proceeds support the South Coast Children's Services. 879-0013.

Harbor Lights Ceremony

A dazzling display of red, green, and white lights reflecting off the water, the camaraderie of the boat owners, and the good humored judging of the "best" decorated boat, makes this an entertaining, and free, holiday event. Held around the middle of December at Pillar Point Harbor. 726-4723.

PERFORMING ARTS AND THEATER

This Side of the Hill Players

The "Players" are an amateur theater group that ambitiously turns out several good plays each year. They are always well done. Generally, there is one grand musical performed during the summer. The This Side of the Hill Players perform at the Mel Mello Center for the Arts, 1167 Main Street in Half Moon Bay. For questions and tickets by phone call: 726-9208. Tickets are also sold at Peggy Erickson's Art Gallery, 726-1598, or Bay Book and Video, 726-3488, in Half Moon Bay.

Pacifica Spindrift Players
Another excellent amateur theater group presents a variety of plays throughout the year. They are located at the Oddstad Theater, 1050 Crespi Drive, Pacifica. To reserve tickets in advance phone: 738-1788.

Bach Dancing and Dynamite Society
This is the establishment on the Coastside with the cleverest name. The Bach offers Sunday afternoon music-by-the-sea held in a rustic wood-sided building perfectly harmonious with the setting and the music. Some of the world's most renown jazz and classical greats are enticed to perform here because of the persuasive powers of the proprietor and because the scenery, setting, and acoustics are so magnificent. Doors open at 3 p.m. Music starts at 4:30 and goes until about 7:30. Located three miles north of Half Moon Bay. Turn towards the ocean at Magellan Avenue in Miramar, and left on Mirada Road. The Douglas Beach House is midway down the block. There is a large parking lot in back of the building. 726-4143.

Enso Center
Unique concerts featuring classical, jazz, and other musical groups are performed the first Friday evening of each month at the Enso Center. 131 Kelly Avenue, Half Moon Bay. 726-1207.

Pacifica Arts and Heritage Council
The Pacifica Arts and Heritage Council sponsors concerts, both classical and jazz, at the Sanchez Arts Center. Children under age 12 are admitted free if accompanied by an adult. The Sanchez Art Center is located in a converted school at 1220 Linda Mar Blvd in Pacifica. 355-1882.

CLUBS AND PUBS

Apple Jacks
Local bands play rock and country music on the weekends in this historic funky bar set in the redwoods. La Honda Road, La Honda. 747-0331

Cameron's Inn
Cameron's hosts a variety of entertainment nights from local folk singers, to comedians, to karaoke, to better-known bands. Audience participation is encouraged. Cameron's is located at 1410 South Highway 1, Half Moon Bay. Call 726-5705 for the latest schedule, or check their website: www.cameronsinn.com.

Ketch Joanne and Harbor Bar.

This is exactly what a bar at the harbor should look like—wood-planked with appropriate sea faring decor. Generally a good lively group gather on the weekends. Pillar Point Harbor, Princeton. 728-3747.

LA DI DA

Live and lively music including blues, folk, rock, and contemporary bands play on Saturdays and Sundays from 11 a.m. to 1 p.m. in this colorful coffee house. 500 C Purissima, Half Moon Bay. 726-1663.

Merry Prankster Café

Bluegrass, country, folk, and other bands play on occasional Saturday evenings and Sunday afternoons. La Honda Road, La Honda. 747-0660

Mezza Luna

Music on the weekends in one of the most comfortable cocktail lounges on the Coast. The large bar is equipped with a dance floor, fireplace, and stage. 459 Prospect Way, Princeton. 728-8108.

Nick's

Live bands play a variety of dance music on the weekends. Nick's is a parking lot away from crashing waves. Rockaway Beach, Pacifica. 359-3900.

Old Princeton Landing

More than a surfer's hangout, they often feature rock and blues bands, usually on the weekends. Famous musicians have been known to show up for a jam session here. 460 Capistrano Road, Princeton. 728-9103.

San Gregorio Store

Weekend afternoons listen to bluegrass, rock and Irish music around the old bar at the San Gregorio Store. Stage Road and Highway 84, San Gregorio. 726-0565

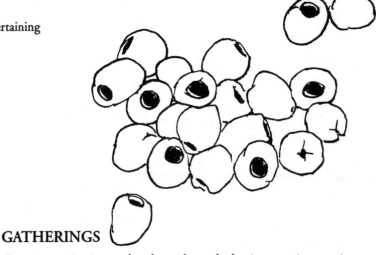

GATHERINGS

Company picnics under the redwoods, brainstorming sessions while overlooking the ocean, birthday parties at a fire station, or weddings in a flower-laden gazebo; whatever the special occasion the Coastside can provide a memorable spot for meeting with friends or associates.

Bed and Breakfasts and Restaurants

Most of the bed and breakfast inns offer minimum meeting space; some, such as the **Seal Cove Inn** (728-4114) in Moss Beach and the **Cypress Inn** (726-6002) in Miramar offer fully equipped meeting rooms. Other inns feature gardens, gazebos, and settings ideal for weddings. Most notable are the **Mill Rose Inn** (726-8750), **Old Thyme Inn** (726-1616), and **San Benito House** (726-3425) in Half Moon Bay. On the South Coast, **Rancho San Gregorio** (747-0810), has a large grassy gazebo area, a tree-shaded picnic grounds equipped with barbecue pits and picnic tables, and a softball field.

Many local restaurants also have private areas for intimate weddings or other gatherings. Check the Eating chapter for a complete description of these facilities.

Conference Centers

The **Half Moon Bay Lodge** has an extensive full-service conference wing offering six meeting rooms, with an in-house conference planner to assist you. This is an excellent choice for business meetings. 2400 South Highway 1, Half Moon Bay. 726-9000; fax: 726-7951.

The Beach House Inn and Conference Center is a very well equipped water-front meeting facility. Four meeting rooms, each with a wood-burning fireplace and some with ocean views, can comfortable seat from 10 to 45 people, more if the terrace is used. 4100 North Highway 1, Half Moon Bay. 712-0220; (800) 315-9366; fax: 712-0693.

Another full service conference facility right on the water, the **Harbor House,** can host weddings and conferences. Catered meals and refreshments and audio/visual equipment available upon request. 346 Princeton Avenue, Princeton. 728-1572; fax: 728-8271.

The Lighthouse Motel has a full-service conference center, with rooms large enough to hold 200 participants banquet style seating. Some meeting rooms have a view of the ocean. An excellent choice for conferences and business meetings, luncheons, or weddings. 105 Rockaway Beach Avenue, Pacifica. 355-6300; (800) 832-4777; fax: 355-9217

Bach Dancing and Dynamite Society is the quintessential "California Beach House" with ocean views, wrap around decks, and plate glass windows. The two rooms and decks overlooking the ocean make "The Bach" ideal for larger parties and weddings. It can accommodate up to 150 people. 311 Mirada Road, Miramar. For business meetings and conferences call Coastside Conference Company, 726-4895. For weddings and receptions call 726-4143.

Strawberry Ranch, a full service conference site, was designed for corporate retreats. It is located at the end of a long dirt road and perched right on the cliffs overlooking the ocean and the greens of the Half Moon Bay Golf Links—a dramatic setting. The per person price includes breakfast and coffee breaks.

Catered lunch can be provided. Located south of Half Moon Bay at the end of Redondo Beach Road. 726-5840, or call Coastside Conference Company at 726-4895.

Enso Gardens is available for groups up to 40 people at this ocean front facility. Food and audio visual equipment are available. 131 Kelly Avenue, Half Moon Bay. 726-1409 or call Coastside Conference Company at 726-4895.

Thomas Fogarty Winery is a spectacular spot to entertain, high in the Northern Santa Cruz Mountains, off Highway 35. The facilities are spacious, modern and offer unsurpassed views. Perfect for all types of business meetings, special events, and weddings. 19501 Skyline Blvd, Woodside. 851-6772.

Unique buildings for special events
How about holding your wedding in an art gallery? At the **Dunn Mehler Gallery** the bride descends a spiral staircase; the vows are given before the picture windows overlooking the surf, and guests are seated among exquisite one-of-a-kind artwork. Limited to 60 guests. 337 Mirada Road, Miramar. 726-7667; fax 726-5977. The **Courtyard Gallery**, 643 Main Street in Half Moon Bay, offers an intimate space for small weddings and parties. 712-7742; fax: 712-1714.

If you want a country club atmosphere for your special event the **Colony Swim and Tennis Club** is a good choice. An atrium room which seats up to 110 people is available. 2000 Fairway Drive, Half Moon Bay. 726-2849.

To rent space with a stage, try the **Mel Mello Center for the Arts**, 1167 Main Street in Half Moon Bay. 726-9208. In Pacifica, the **Oddstad Theater** offers limited space for weddings and other group events. The theater is an attractive, older building in a woodland setting. Lighted parking lot. 1050 Crespi Drive, Pacifica. 738-7380.

A lighthouse perched on the ocean's edge is a splendid place for a wedding or special event. Both the **Pigeon Point Lighthouse**, 879-0633, and the **Montara Lighthouse**, 728-7177, can accommodate groups for day or evening events.

Other unique buildings equipped to handle special events include the **Bell Building**, a converted switching office for Pacific Bell, now a spacious all-events room with a kitchen and bar for up to 219 people. 565 Kelly Avenue, Half Moon Bay. 726-0223. **Pedro Point Firehouse** is a refurbished firehouse available for wedding receptions and parties. Danmann Avenue in Pacifica. 355-4726. **Montara Gardens** has been a school and is now an attractive building and gardens offering several areas for groups. 496 Sixth Street, Montara. 728-7442.

Outdoor Venues

Cozzolino Park is nestled in a grove of trees offering a relaxing setting for company picnics and informal weddings. The picnic tables seat up to 160 people. The privately owned area has parking, covered barbecue pits, dance floor, electricity, volleyball court, and bathrooms. Located east of Half Moon Bay at 12001 Highway 92. 726-4383.

One of the few gated beaches on the mid-coast, **Sweetwood Park**, is a reservations only beach and is often used for company picnics, scout overnights, and large beach parties. It is a part of the Half Moon Bay State Park system and is located off Highway 1, north of Half Moon Bay. (800) 444-7275.

La Honda Gardens has a large grassy area, encircled by redwood trees, an especially attractive spot for company picnics or performances. There is a stage with electricity and temporary restrooms. La Honda Road, La Honda. 747-0896.

Old cypress,
north of Half Moon Bay
on Highway 1

9

SHOPPING

The hub of shopping activity on the Coastside is Half Moon Bay. The tree and flower-lined Main Street, with its gas street lamps and brightly painted turn-of-the-century buildings, is a browser's delight. But Half Moon Bay is a true town not just a tourist mecca. On Main Street art galleries, antique stores, and gift shops exist alongside grocery and lighting stores, veterinarian hospitals, and optometrists.

South of Half Moon Bay, in San Gregorio, Pescadero, Davenport, and La Honda the adventurous shopper will be rewarded with some unusual finds at some unusual shops. North of Half Moon Bay, Pacifica has a collection of shopping centers, but no real downtown. Several of their stores are worth a stop.

Most of the shops on the Coastside are open Monday through Saturday from 10 a.m. to 5 p.m. Some are also open from noon to 5 p.m. on Sunday. If in doubt, call ahead. We begin our shopping spree in Half Moon Bay. Then we travel to the Mid-Coast, the South Coast, and Pacifica in that order.

HALF MOON BAY

Main Street

Main Street is located on the east side of Highway 1 and intersects Highway 92. The best way to enjoy Main Street is to walk up one side and down the other, poking your head in the various shops. There is on-street parking and a number of parking lots off of Main Street and on Mill Street in back of the Tin Palace.

Start at the **Stone Pine Shopping Center** located just south of the corner of Main Street and Highway 92. **Half Moon Bay Coffee Company** (726-3664) is the cornerstone to the Stone

Pine Center. The very fine **Moon News** (726-8610) sells newspapers and magazines from around the globe, as well as a good selection of books. Create your own pottery at **Main Street Pottery** (726-7675) or satisfy your sporting needs at **Half Moon Bay Sports and Golf Center** (712-9900) and **The Bike Works** (726-6708).

Walk across the wooden bridge to the **Tin Palace** at 315 Main Street. Located in a reconverted auto repair shed, the Tin Palace houses restaurants, specialty shops, and an "artist's walk," a changing display of local artist's work. The **Buffalo Shirt Company** (726-3194) is the anchor store and an exceptionally fine shop selling Coastside casual clothing. They have a good variety of Pendleton clothing and other premier labels. Next door, the **Paper Crane** (726-0722) is a purveyor of cards, gifts, children's toys, and books. Leave yourself plenty of time to linger. You never know what treasure you will find in this delightful shop. Letterpress printing is meticulously done behind the counter while you watch. Next to the Tin Palace is a small but compelling compact disk shop called the **Music Hut** (726-8742) with a wide selection of music, both CD's and tapes.

Also on the 300 block of Main Street, **Half Moon Bay Feed and Fuel** (726-4814) is an authentic farm supply store selling saddles, boots, rabbits, chickens, all kinds of pet supplies, animal feed, and farm implements. The wooden floors and country western music playing in the background add to the great old-time, rural atmosphere. **Arrigotti Fine Jewelry** (726-0248) designs and crafts jewelry to your specifications.

Notice the wonderful clock on the 400 block of Main Street as you browse in **Damsel In A Dress** (726-4327), featuring hip women's clothing; **Ambiance** (560-9844), an upscale furniture and antique shop; and **Cooking Sensations** (712-0144), purveyors of quality cookware. The 500 block houses an eclectic collection of boutiques: **Calico Barn** (726-9646) sells teddy bears and other appealing handicrafts; **P. Cottontail** (726-0200) sells a fine selection of children's clothing; **Tokenz** (712-8457) is the place to go for inexpensive gifts, beads, and unusual jewelry; and **Main Street Goldworks** (726-2546) crafts handmade jewelry on the premises.

Half to Have It, Main Street Exchange (712-5995) is on the corner of Main and Kelly Streets and is an outdoor bazaar of antiques, garden furnishings, and old objects. **Cottage Industries** (712-8078) sells Amish, Shaker and European rustic furniture; **Plum Tree Corner**, located at Main and Correas Streets, houses stores with an artistic bent: **Textures** (712-4408)sells wearable art and **Couryard Gallery** (712-7742) is a petite fine arts gallery.

Cross Main Street and go down the other side.
La Piazza, on the corner of Main and Miramontes Streets, is a European-style enclosed shopping plaza and an another amazing refurbishment of an auto repair garage. At the entrance is **Moonside Bakery and Café** (726-9070) and **Garden Gallery** (712-1949), selling traditional paintings by California's contemporary artists, including some work by locals. Robert Dvorák, the artist for this book, exhibits his paintings at this gallery. The **Half Moon Bay Wine and Cheese Shop** (726-1520) can be a tasty stop for wine tasting and sampling their wide selection of cheeses. Other shops include **Sterling Road** (712-0643), a silversmith, **Cece's Bridal Shop** (726-3840), and the **Coastal Hemp Company** (712-9292), selling environmentally correct goods all made from hemp.

In the 500 block of Main Street, **Peggy Erikson Art and Framing** (726-1598) sells original paintings and limited edition prints and posters featuring Coastside artists. Stop at **M. Coffee's** (726-6241), an atmospheric and longtime coffee house favorite, and **Half Moon Bay Bakery** (726-4841) for a cup of java and a little snack along this block of Main Street. Next

door, **Pescadero II** (726-7864) sells brightly colored t-shirts, hand-painted silk scarves, and other coastside handicrafts that are wonderful keepsakes of the coast.

Enter **Cunha's Country Store** (726-4071), on the 400 block of Main Street, and the mixed aromas smell so good you want to stay. Upstairs rummage through everything from cowboy boots to shelf paper. Downstairs lunch on great sandwiches, local produce, Portuguese specialties, and Mexican pastries. Next to Cunha's Store, upstairs, is the **Gallery of Native American Creations** (726-6723), featuring an expansive inventory of Native American arts and crafts. Further along find **Coastside Books** (726-5889), a comfortable and complete bookstore, and **Coastal Comforts** (726-3600) selling bath and bedroom amenities. The **Coastal Gallery** (726-3859) is in an alley-way so don't overlook this fine art gallery showing original oils, water colors, sculpture pieces, prints, and posters. Some local artists' works are on display. **Magazzi** (726-4021)sells unusual and often exciting women's clothing and jewelry, and the **Charmed Rose** (712-1622) is a handicrafts consignment shop. **Ocean Books** (726-2665) is a used bookstore with a handsome library setting. Browse for books in this shop and pick up many tidbits of information about the Coastside from the many patrons and the owner. **Quail Run** (726-3112) well displays and sells nature related gifts with a garden and coastside floral bent; **Harbor Seal Company** (726-7418) specializes in a fine selection of marine, nature, and wildlife clothing, toys and gifts. **Hand Spun Gallery** (726-2550) has a spinning wheel in action as well as beautiful yarns, blankets, and toys.

Zaballa Square, in 300 Main Street block, houses upscale furniture stores, art galleries, and other specialty shops. **Briggs and Riley** (712-7700) is a local manufacturer of handsome luggage carrying unlimited lifetime warranties; stop by to enjoy this well appointed showroom. Travel togs and accessories are also sold by a knowledgeable staff. **Cartwheels** (726-6060) and **Gallery M** (726-7167) both carry an outstanding selection of unusual furniture. **Light and Art** (726-3080) has a fine blown glass inventory, and the **Galleria Luna** (726-8932) displays fine art. **Lunar Wind Inventions** (726-9212) sells kites; visit **Seascapes** (712-8096) for your gifts from the sea and local souvenirs. **The Coastal Art League Museum and Sales** (726-6335) shows and sells works by their members as well as invited artists. They also sponsor art destination tours. Open weekends from 11 a.m. to 5 p.m.

On the North end of Main Street, north of Highway 92, **A Bicyclery** (726-6000) has a wide selection of bicycles and accessories and does repairs. On South Main Street, **The Gingerbread Barn** (726-6644) carries a large selection of early American decorations including some hard-to-find handmade dolls, rocking chairs, and benches to seat them. They also teach tole painting classes and sell all of the books and paraphernalia needed.

Kelly Avenue

The **Mirren Gallery** (712-1320) displays a range of fine art and sculpture in a cottage setting at 510 Kelly Avenue. Walk down the driveway to the side of the gallery to the **Old Alves Dairy Barn**, a studio for local artisans. **Kelly Avenue Potters** (726-8628) and **Randall Reid Ceramics** (726-7689) both specialize in functional and decorative pottery; **Pacific Patio** (726-3650) builds custom redwood patio furniture. Across from Kelly Avenue, at 225 South Cabrillo Highway, is the **Spring Mountain Gallery** (726-3025) displaying photographs and unique framing.

Spanishtown Art & Craft Center

Spanishtown (726-9971) is one of the few arts-only complexes in California. It is a crafts fair in miniature located in a rustic barn setting. A variety of unique shops surround a courtyard and offer all kinds of gifts, handmade crafts, pottery, jewelry, art, and antiques. The center is open every weekend. Some shops are also open Wednesday to Friday afternoons. Highway 92, half mile east of Half Moon Bay.

Strawflower Shopping Center

This shopping center is located at the junction of Highway 1 and Highway 92 and includes some of the town's large chain stores as well as the following more individual shops: **Bay Book and Video** (726-3488) is one of the best stocked bookstores in the Bay Area with exceptionally helpful clerks. There is a good selection of best sellers, fantasy, science fiction, travel books and many other subjects. **Lady Bug, Lady Bug** (726-1726) sells pretty, fashionable ladies clothing and accessories. **Pumpkin Patch Hallmark**(726-3488) carries a large selection of Coastside souvenirs and **Sea Squirts** (726-1139) can supply all the toys you need.

MID-COAST

Every shopping trip to the Coastside should include a stop at **Dunn Mehler Gallery** (726-7667) in Miramar. Go to see the contemporary building, the exquisite beach side location, and fine selection of sculptures, ceramics, and other three dimensional art pieces. 337 Mirada Road. Open daily except Tuesday. Nearby Pillar Point Harbor is home to a few rustic and rather funky antique and gift shops, located on Capistrano Road.

In Moss Beach you might want to hunt up **Remembrance**, a collector's store. The somewhat frayed exterior belies the beautiful, handcrafted toys, stuffed animals, wooden objects, and Christmas tree ornaments sold within. Open daily. 570 Vermont Street, Moss Beach.

SOUTH COAST

Journey back in time and enter the **San Gregorio General Store** (726-0565). This country store carries everything from classic farm needs to Estonian Cookbooks and an especially wide selection of ecological books. A country pub bar dominates the front of the store, and a wood-burning stove provides a comfortable setting for a cup of coffee and a book. Stage Road at Highway 84, San Gregorio.

A walk around Pescadero will yield a few interesting shops. **Country Roads Antique Store** (879-0452) sells a wide selection of quilts, antiques, and pine furniture on Stage Road, Pescadero. **Norm's Market** (879-0147) sells just-out-of-the-oven breads. The old west style building provides the right atmosphere for the good stock of wines and picnic items as well as regular staples. Stage Road, Pescadero.

Continue on Highway 84 to La Honda to find **La Honda Creations Craft Gallery** (747-0965), a very fine gallery selling pottery by local artists, handcrafted jewelry, and clothing. Find out about the local lore from the owner. Closed Mondays.

137

Davenport has become something of an artists colony as well as a satisfying shopping experience. **Davenport Cash Store** (408) 425-1818 sells unusual pottery, handcrafted jewelry, bolts of bright colored fabric from South America, and local arts and crafts. It is worth a trip to Davenport to dine in the adjacent restaurant and browse in this unique shop. Located at the corner of Highway 1 and Davenport Avenue. **Omware Glass Studio** (408) 429-5307, located at 500 B, Highway 1, sells one of a kind kiln-fired functional glassware and hand dipped candles by local artists. Open daily.

It's odd to find a world renown art glass studio in Davenport, but **Lundberg Studios**, (408) 423-2532, produces exquisite paper weights and other art glass items sold worldwide. If your pocket book isn't up to world class spending, ask to see their garage where they sell seconds. Located at 131 Old Coast Road. Around the corner, find **David Boye Knives Gallery**, (408) 426-6046, at 111-B Marine View Avenue. Besides the exceptionally beautiful handcrafted knives sold here, find scrimshaw, jewelry, and hardwood craft items. **Whale Hedge Studio**, (408) 458-1959, at 51 Ocean Street in Davenport, has a real whale hedge in front, and sells the work of a local watercolorist.

PACIFICA

Pacifica is a collection of nine small villages, joined together in 1957 to form one linear community. This means there is no downtown Pacifica. Most of the tourist oriented shops are located in Rockaway Beach, off Highway 1. At 205 Rockaway, you will find **Antiques and Collectibles** (738-1934), **Christmas by the Cove** (355-2683), and **Carousel Classics** (355-3359), gifts and souvenirs from around the World. At the Roackaway Beach Plaza, 450 Rockaway, find **Hanni's Fine Gifts** (359-4721), and hand-painted woman's clothing, lighthouse ornaments, wooden sea birds, sea shells. **Paul Strom** (355-5553) is an exceptional hair, skin and body care saloon.

The **Sanchez Art Center** (355-1894) is a unique gallery, showing the works of local and guest artists from the Bay Area. Several artists rent studios and work on the premises including the artist for this book, Robert Dvorák. Sculptures, paintings, and other types of art are on display. Open Fridays from 1 p.m. to 5 p.m., and Saturdays and Sundays, 11 a.m. to 4 p.m. Located at 1220 Linda Mar Blvd in a remodeled school.

Eureka Square, off Oceana Blvd, houses the excellent **Pacifica Book Company** (738-9000), selling new books, gifts, and stationery. Also in Eureka Square, **A Bicyclery** (738-1800) sells and repairs bicycles. In Manor Plaza, a shopping center off Manor Drive, collectors of handicrafts will want to go to **Relatively Crafty** (355-5903), a crafts and collectibles consignment shop that also sells craft supplies. Another Pacifica Bookstore, **Florey's** (355-8811), is off the beaten track located in the downstairs of an apartment building. Inside you will find a maze of rooms, each filled with a bright display of books, unique greeting cards, and small gift items. 2316 Palmetto.

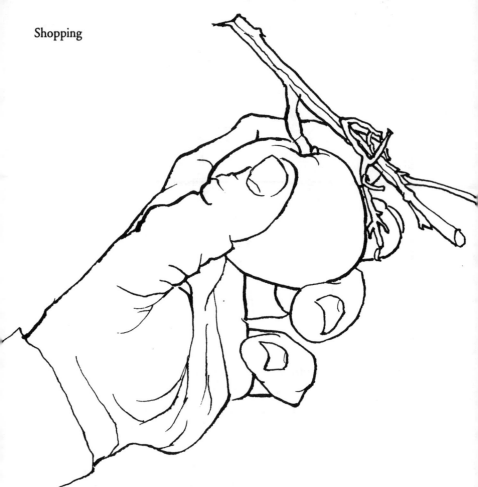

GROWING AND HARVESTING

Shop in nature's own mall. In October find the perfect pumpkin from the sea of orange spheres covering the fields. Then come back one month later to smell the sweet, sticky pinesap as you cut your own Christmas tree. The rest of the year there are olallieberries (a variety of blackberries), strawberries, and kiwifruit to be picked. Choose from artichokes, peas, Brussels sprouts, and flowers straight from the fields.

The Coastside is rich in its variety of vegetables, fruits, Christmas trees, and of course, pumpkins. There are several good establishments selling the coastal bounty. Prices are competitive and in many cases very inexpensive. The information is arranged by product, beginning with the biggest local stars: pumpkins and cut-your-own Christmas trees.

Pumpkin Patches and Christmas Tree Farms
Most of the pumpkin patches and Christmas tree farms are found along Highway 92 east of Half Moon Bay and on Highway 1 between Half Moon Bay and Año Nuevo. Generally the pumpkin patches are open daily from the first of October. Christmas tree farms are open daily from the day after Thanksgiving. Some of the pumpkin patches and Christmas tree farms have become event destinations offering pony rides, good things to eat, and a real holiday atmosphere. Two of the most popular are just across from each other on Highway 92, east of Half Moon Bay.

Just follow the traffic any day in October through December to **Pastorino Farms** (726-6440). This is the place to come for a festive display of Halloween and Christmas fun. Beginning the last part of September until Halloween pick your own pumpkins, take hay, train and pony rides, and sample all manner of pumpkin goods. Ideal for school groups. Beginning the first of December until Christmas, you can buy fresh cut Christmas trees, poinsettias, tree ornaments, and visit Santa Claus on weekends. Highway 92, east of Half Moon Bay.

Just across Highway 92 from Pastorino Farms, **Lemos** (726-2342) is also open daily during the holiday periods with a variety of pumpkins and cut-your-own Christmas trees. At Halloween, the barn becomes a haunted house. Hay rides, pony rides, and farm animals are festively available. In December the buildings are covered with Christmas decorations.

Arata Pumpkin & Animal Farm (726-4359) also has farm animals and pony rides for entertainment. Call first for an appointment. Four miles south of Half Moon Bay on Highway 1, before Martin's Beach.

Fruits and Vegetables

As you might expect, there are several fresh fruit and vegetable stands in Half Moon Bay, along the Mid-Coast, and on the South Coast. Many of these are located along Highway 92 and Highway 1 outside of Half Moon Bay.

Andreotti Family Farm (726-9461) sells fresh local produce, many organically grown, from one of the coast's most picturesque barns. Often rabbits, goats, turkeys, or other small farm animals are on display outside the barn. The family grows their own artichokes, herbs, tomatoes, and other crops. Open weekends. 331 Kelly Avenue, Half Moon Bay.

The Farmer's Daughter grows and sells organically grown vegetables including fresh peas, artichokes, and white corn. Open weekends during growing seasons. On Highway 1 across from the airport, between El Granada and Moss Beach.

Pardini's sells fresh vegetables, fruits, and nursery stock. There is a good selection of begonias, bougainvillea, and fuchsias. Open weekends during the summer months. Located in Princeton-by-the-Sea, on Prospect Avenue.

Phipps Ranch (879-0787) is no garden variety vegetable stand. It is a destination in its own right for picnicking, farm animals, exotic birds, and a wide variety of local produce. Shop

for fruits and vegetables, dried herbs, and flowers and nursery items. From June to August pick your own strawberries, raspberries, and olallieberries. Open daily. 2700 Pescadero Road.

Return to your farm roots at **Coastways Ranch** (879-0414). Pick your own olallieberries in June and July, pumpkins in October, and kiwifriut and Christmas trees in November and December. You also can buy artichokes, flowers, Brussels sprouts and other local specialties. School and group tours are by appointment. Open Wednesday to Sunday during picking seasons. Call ahead for hours and exact picking dates. Highway 1, 30 miles south of Half Moon Bay.

Gift Baskets
The Pigeon Point Company (879-0126; (800) 919-0126) is a unique company that produces gift baskets filled with products made or grown on the coastside. Ceramic honey pots, charming cottage gift boxes, beeswax candles, chocolate fudge mustard, lavender sachets, and other unique items go into these one-of-a-kind baskets produced in a barn in Pescadero. Open to visitors by appointment.

Wineries
Obester Winery (726-9463) is a family-run winemaker and bottler of prize-winning wines. You can stop in for a tasting, and bring a picnic lunch to enjoy the comfortable surroundings. They are best known for their Chardonnay, Sauvignon Blanc, and Johannesburg Riesling. The shop and tasting rooms are open daily. Highway 92, two miles east of Half Moon Bay.

Thomas Fogarty Winery (851-6777) commands one of the most stunning views in the Bay Area. Fortunately, the public is encouraged to enjoy the tasting room, or rent the California style wood and glass facilities for business conferences, weddings, and other private gatherings. Estate Pinot Noir, Chardonnay, and Merlot are their specialties. Open Thursday to Sunday, 11 a.m. to 5 p.m. 19501 Skyline Blvd, Woodside.

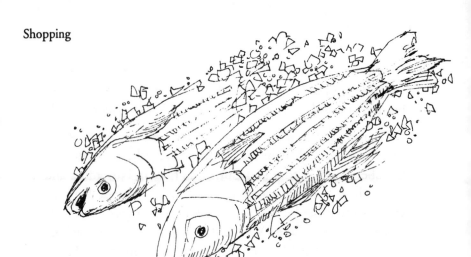

Fresh Fish

If you want to take the local catch of the day home with you, go to the Pillar Point Harbor, four miles north of Half Moon Bay. Year round fish is sold directly off the boats in the harbor. Call the **Fishermen's Hotline** at 712-0252 for a recorded message touting the day's catch.

Also at the harbor, **The Princeton Seafood Company** (726-2722) sells fresh fish daily. They will filet and clean the fish and pack it in ice for your trip home. **The Fresh Fish House** (728-5538; (800) 52-Fish-9) also sells just-from-the-ocean fish. Open daily. 230 Princeton Avenue, Princeton.

Nurseries

There are several commercial flower growers on the Coastside. Most of them are for the wholesale trade only. The following nurseries are open to the public:

Several nurseries are located on Highway 92, east of Half Moon Bay; they are all open daily. The greenhouses of the **Half Moon Bay Nursery** (726-5392) explode with color. The pink, reds, oranges, and whites of the geraniums, fuchsias, tuberous begonias, and bougainvillea are worthy of a trip. The nursery carries a large variety of coastal plants, many grown on the property. This is simply one of the best nurseries in the Bay Area.

Bongards Treescape Nursery (726-4568) provides a very good stock of ornamental trees and scrubs, bedding plants, and ground cover. **Cozzolino's Floral Design and Nursery** (726-4383) sells bedding plants and scrubs, as well as cut flowers and arrangements from a greenhouse.

Flora Farm Nursery (726-9223) is hidden away on a side street in downtown Half Moon Bay behind the Zaballa House, at 340 Purisima Street. Bedding plants, herbs, and miniature plants are sold from a small rustic barn.

Go Native Nursery (728-2286) and the **Cypress Flower Farm** (728-0728) also operate out of a picturesque barn located at 333 Cypress Avenue in Moss Beach. Go Native Nursery is a retail nursery specializing in California native plants; Cypress Flower Farm sells cut flowers, house plants, and gifts.

The **Shelldance Bromeliad and Orchid Nursery** (355-4845) is one of the largest and most complete bromeliad nurseries in the country and grows more than 600 varieties of exotic colorful bromeliads. Open weekdays from 8:30 a.m. to 4:30 p.m. 2000 Highway l, Pacifica.

Yerba Buena Nursery (851-1668) is one of California's oldest retail native plant nurseries. It is a little out of the way, but the surroundings are magnificent and the friendly staff encourages you to explore. Finish your walking tour at the Tea Terrace, the nursery's own tea room, for a cup of herbal tea or spiced cider. Located at 19500 Skyline Blvd in Woodside across from Thomas Fogarty Winery. Drive two miles down a narrow dirt road to the nursery. **Farwell's Rhododendron Nursery** (851-8812) is also located on Skyline Blvd, at 13040 Skyline. Rhododendron of all sizes, types, and colors have been grown and sold here since 1946. Closed the month of July and on all holidays.

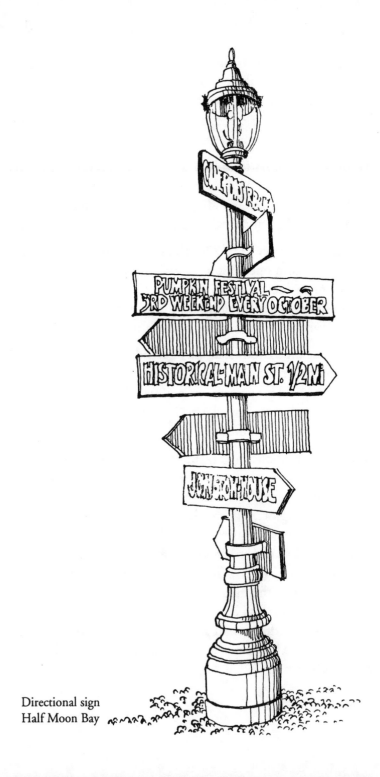

Directional sign
Half Moon Bay

10

INFORMING

Visitors to the San Mateo coast soon sense the slower pace and relaxing mood stimulated by the ocean, mountains, open fields, and village-like towns. This chapter is a brief directory of important and helpful telephone numbers.

GETTING AROUND

Auto
Highway l, also known as the Coast Highway or Cabrillo Highway, is the main north-south artery along the San Mateo coast. Sharp Park Boulevard and Highways 92 and 84 are the east-west connecting roads to Highway l. Most of these roads are narrow and congested; but relax, this can give you the opportunity to view the impressive farmland, mountains, and beaches.

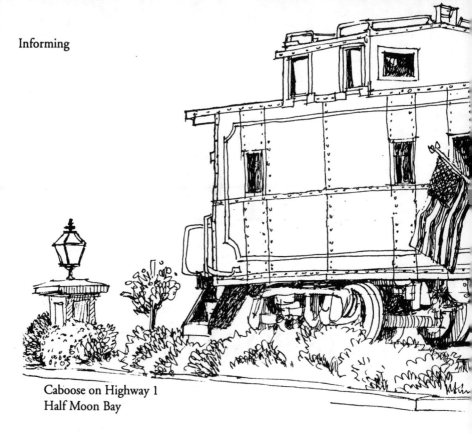

Caboose on Highway 1
Half Moon Bay

Car Rentals
Enterprise Rent-a-Car is located at 213 San Mateo Road, Suite 12, Half Moon Bay. 712-6880.

Bus
SamTrans buses travel between Half Moon Bay, Pacifica, and the Daly City BART Station; Half Moon Bay and Hillsdale Shopping Center; and Half Moon Bay and Año Nuevo State Reserve. Pacifica has more frequent bus service. Call SamTrans for schedules. (800) 660-4287.

Taxi
Two taxi cab companies service the entire Coastside and are especially useful for airport transfers. Coast Cab Company: 738-8000; (800) 303-TAXI, and Pacifica City Cab Company: 359-2290.

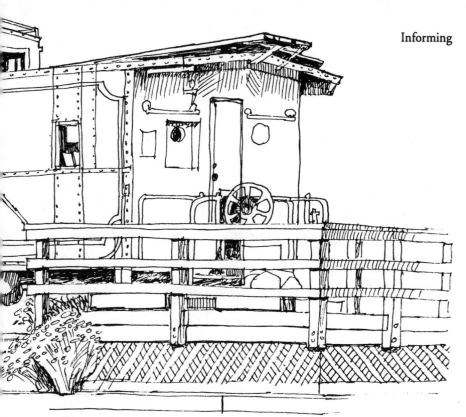

Limousine
For limousine service call California Pacific Limousine (726-2664 or 738-5668), Coastside-A Plus Limousine (728-5466), and Gateway Limousine (726-1504).

Boats
Boats arriving at Pillar Point Harbor can anchor out between the inner and outer breakwater. Call the Harbor Master at 726-4382 for exact mooring locations. The local Half Moon Bay Yacht Club can be reached at 728-2120. Its facilities are available for use by members of other yacht clubs.

Air
The Half Moon Bay Airport, located between El Granada and Moss Beach along Highway 1, is used by small aircraft. The airport operates seven days a week and offers overnight tie-down service. 573-3701.

EMERGENCY NUMBERS

In case of an emergency always call 911 first. This gets the police, fire, and ambulance service all alerted at once.

Police

Half Moon Bay Police: 726-8288

San Mateo County Sheriff's Office: 726-4435

Pacifica Police: 738-7314

Highway Patrol (Pacifica):   day: 369-6261

night: (707) 648-5550

Fire and Rescue

Half Moon Bay Fire: 726-5213

El Granada Fire: 726-4422

Montara and Moss Beach Fire: 728-3022

La Honda Volunteer Fire Brigade: 747-0381

Pescadero Fire: 879-0121

Pacifica Fire: 738-7362

Hospital

Seton Coastside Hospital (Emergency Room): Marine Blvd and Etheldore Street, Moss Beach. 728-5521

Emergency ambulance: 364-1313

Poison Control Center: (800) 523-2222

Animal Assistance
Peninsula Humane Society: 340-8200

Department of Fish and Game (District Office): 688-6340

(State Office): (916)653-7664

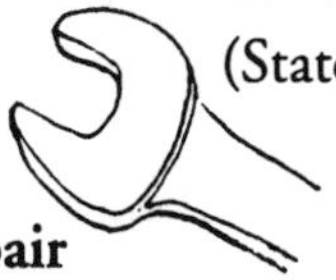

Emergency Auto Repair
Twenty-four hour tow service: Curley and Red's Body Shop and Auto Repair in Half Moon Bay. 726-4027.

Hack's Auto Body and Towing in Pacifica. 359-1941

USEFUL INFORMATION

Half Moon Bay Chamber of Commerce
Open weekdays from 10 a.m. to 4 p.m. Closed from 12 to 1 p.m. daily. 520 Kelly Ave, Half Moon Bay. 726-5202 and 726-8380. Website: www.halfmoonbaychamber.org

Pacifica Chamber of Commerce
Open weekdays 9 a.m. to 5 p.m.; weekends and holidays 10 a.m. to 4:30 p.m. 225 Rockaway Beach Avenue, Suite 1, Pacifica. 355-4122. Website: www.pacificachamber.com

Princeton Harbor Master: 726-4382

Local Parks
Half Moon Bay Parks and Recreation: 726-8297

Pacifica Beaches and Recreation: 875-7380

Golden Gate National Recreational Area
Milagra Ridge Park: 556-8371

Sweeney Ridge: (415) 239-2366

County Parks
San Mateo County Parks and Recreation: 363-4020

Reservations for San Mateo County Parks: 363-4021

San Mateo County Parks:

James V. Fitzgerald Marine Reserve: 728-3584

Pescadero Park: 879-0238

San Mateo Memorial County Park: 879-0238

Sam McDonald Park: 879-0238

San Pedro Valley Park: 355-8289

Sanchez Adobe: 359-1462

State Parks
California State Parks and Beaches information: 726-6238;

San Mateo Coast District Office (California State Parks): 726-6203

Reservations for State Parks: (800) 444-7275

California State Parks and Beaches:

Año Nuevo State Reserve: 879-0227; (800) 444-4445

NEWSPAPERS

Half Moon Bay Review
Weekly newspaper for Half Moon Bay, the Mid-Coast and the South Coast: 726-4424

Coast Views Magazine
Free monthly magazine covering events on the Coast: 726-0307. website: www.coastviewmag.com

The Pacifica Tribune
Weekly newspaper for Pacifica: 359-6666. e-mail: pactrib@hax.com

USEFUL WEBSITES

www.coastside.net for many details on the Coast.

ww.coastsidehomeguide.com for real estate on the Coast

www.montara.com for local issues on the mid-Coast

www.southcoast.net for South Coast news

www.park-net.com and www.cal-parks.ca.gov for California Department of Parks and Recreation

www.dot.ca.gov for CalTrans road conditions

www.youcreate.com for Robert Dvorak's website

www.worldviewbooks.com for updates on this book

AREA AND ZIP CODES
THE AREA CODE FOR HALF MOON BAY AND THE SAN MATEO COAST IS 650

Coastal zip codes:

Half Moon Bay: 94019

El Granada: 94018

Moss Beach: 94038

Montara: 94037

San Gregorio: 94074

Pescadero: 94060

La Honda: 94020

Davenport: 95017

Pacifica: 94044

POST OFFICES

Half Moon Bay, 500 Stone Pine Road. 726-5517.

El Granada, 20 Avenida Portola. 726-5000.

Moss Beach, Highway 1. 728-3151.

Montara, Seventh and Main Streets. 728-5251.

San Gregorio, San Gregorio Road. 726-1045.

Pescadero, 2020 Pescadero Road. 879-0214.

La Honda, La Honda Road. 747-0515.

Pacifica, 50 West Manor Drive. 355-4000; (800) 275-8777.

690 Roberts Road. 359-2661; (800) 275-8777.

PUBLIC RESTROOMS

All the State Beaches and Parks up and down the coast have restroom facilities. Usually the ranger will allow you to park for a few minutes to use the restroom without charge. In addition there are public restrooms at:

Half Moon Bay

Mac Dutra Park, corner of Main Street and Kelly Avenue.

Zaballa Square on Main Street

El Granada

Johnson Pier at Pillar Point Harbor in Princeton.

Moss Beach

James V. Fitzgerald Marine Reserve. Turn west on California Avenue off Highway 1 to North Lake Street.

Montara

Montara Beach, south of The Chart House on Highway 1.

Pacifica

Pacifica Municipal Pier, Beach Blvd and Santa Rosa Avenue.

Pacifica State Beach, Highway 1 between Crespi and Linda Mar Blvd.

INDEX

ORDER FORM

To order this book directly from the publishers, please send a check or money order to:

Worldview Associates, Inc.

P.O. Box 819

El Granada, CA 94018

Phone & Fax: 650-726-7114

e-mail: Nevans@best.com

Visit us at our website: www.worldviewbooks.com

Please send _____copies of *Half Moon Bay Exploring*. Price: $12.95

Please send _____copies of *Monterey Bay Exploring*. Price: $14.95

Shipping and handling:
Add $2 for the first book and $1 for each additional book ordered.
For all books shipped to California addresses, add 8.25% tax.

Amount enclosed:_____

Autographed to:_____

Shipped to:
Name_____

Address_____

City_____

State, Zip_____

ASK US ABOUT QUANTITY DISCOUNTS